"Beckhard has done it again! He sets out to tell us a story—his own—and along the way passes on his great wisdom. He truly is a master teacher; using the unfolding of his life and career, he teaches us how to be flexible, develop theory from practice, garner strength through experience, create change, and much more. Every chapter is filled with Dick's anecdotes and learnings—our lessons so to speak. He clearly "walks his talk," creating a context for our own learning.

I have known "Professor Beckhard" during the family business portion of his long career. Although I knew about his past careers, I was astounded to learn how he was able to move so deftly from one career to another and then within one career from one interest to another. It is a skill that the next generation will need as they move along in the information age. The subtext of these career moves gives us much knowledge and insight into not only the man but also a way of thinking, approaching tasks, developing new concepts and techniques. Anyone who has been associated with him has constantly marveled at these abilities and has tried valiantly to keep up.

It is clear to me that the development of the family business field and the Family Firm Institute were natural outgrowths of Beckhard's rich life experiences. From his early "work" with his father in his business to his own entrepreneurial endeavors, he evolved into his interest and focus in this area. I was pleased to see him make explicit his method of working with family business clients, one that is certainly befitting his life cycle stage of confidant/advisor to the CEO. Dick has continued to share his insights, suggestions, and provocations with both the membership and leadership of the field. Our own and the future generations of family business consultants, teachers, and business owners will find themselves enhanced by this book, both personally and professionally."

—Fredda Herz Brown, Ph.D., *principal,*
The Metropolitan Group

Agent of Change

Richard Beckhard

Agent of Change

My Life, My Practice

Jossey-Bass Publishers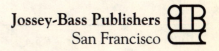
San Francisco

The Commitment and Responsibility Charts in Appendix B are from R. Beckhard/ R. Harris, *Organizational Transitions*, (figs. 9-1 & 9-2 from pages 95 & 105). © 1987 Addison-Wesley Publishing Company Inc. Reprinted by permission of Addison-Wesley Longman Inc.

Appendix C is from "The Confrontation Meeting" by Richard Beckhard, March–April 1967. Copyright © 1967 by the President and Fellows of Harvard College; all rights reserved. Reprinted by permission of *Harvard Business Review*.

Substantial discounts on bulk quantities of Jossey-Bass books are available to corporations, professional associations, and other organizations. For details and discount information, contact the special sales department at Jossey-Bass Inc., Publishers (415) 433-1740; Fax (800) 605-2665.

For sales outside the United States, please contact your local Simon & Schuster International Office.

Jossey-Bass Web address: http://www.josseybass.com

Manufactured in the United States of America on Lyons Falls Turin Book. This paper is acid-free and 100 percent totally chlorine-free.

Library of Congress Cataloging-in-Publication Data

Beckhard, Richard, date.
   Agent of change : my life, my practice / Richard Beckhard.
     p. cm.—(The Jossey-Bass business & management series)
   Includes index.
   ISBN 0-7879-1012-0
   1. Beckhard, Richard, date. 2. Business consultants—United States—Biography. 3. Organizational change—United States.
4. Interpersonal relations—United States. 5. Management—United States. I. Title. II. Series.
HD69.C6B43 1997
001'.092—dc21
[B]
                                   97-21159
                                   CIP

HB Printing   10 9 8 7 6 5 4 3 2 1   FIRST EDITION

The Jossey-Bass
Business & Management Series

Dedicated to Sandra Barty and to all the colleagues, practitioners, and students who are the future of the work described in this book.

Contents

Resources

Preface

For the past several years, and with increasing frequency, friends, colleagues, ex-students, and clients have been giving or sending me a message: "You've had a tremendous amount of experience. You ought to write about it." Certainly, the first statement is true. I've been an organization consultant for forty-seven of my seventy-nine years. But the second statement demanded action. At my age, was it action on which I wanted to expend valuable time? I have been extremely fortunate in the work I have been able to do. I have also been honored more than I can deserve, by my colleagues, students, and clients. What additional value would such writing provide— and for whom?

The argument for it is that my vast and varied experience is, in itself, something that people who are struggling with the kinds of issues I have worked with for so long can use in their development. In short, if wisdom is the combination of knowledge plus experience, I have some wisdom that would be worth sharing.

It's a flattering concept. But flattery was not what I needed. What I needed was to know if writing my professional memoirs would result in something that was truly useful to others. Passing on something of value has long been a concern of mine. Fifteen years ago, as part of a learning workshop, I was asked to respond to the question, If you could have achieved totally what you want to be and do professionally, what would you have done? I found, somewhat to my surprise, that I had no difficulty answering the question. I want to influence organizations to function in a more humane as well as high-performing mode. I want to have been significant in empowering the next generation of people with the same goal.

At the time, the workshop statement made explicit to me the criteria I would use in choosing my professional activities. For me to take an assignment, I would have to feel that it furthered at least one of these goals. In retrospect, those criteria then guided my practice—and eventually guided me to write this book.

The effort involved—reliving and reflecting on my career, writing, and rewriting—has brought to mind many stories. It has helped me to organize the richness of my memories into some useful categories: the major learnings and their potential applications from my forty-nine years of work in the field. I have had a lot of experience, much of it worth sharing. Beyond that, I have done a lot of experiencing, much of which is even more valuable. Indeed, as I have learned, the process, the doing, has been key.

My life pattern has consistently been one of doing something because it was there to be done and then trying to learn from the doing. For me, the only way of learning is by doing. In contrast, the traditional practice in development is linear. First you learn how to do something. Then when you have learned enough, you do it. I can't personally recommend that method. I never did anything because I was prepared for it.

In high school, I became a drama critic by being one when the local critic was sick. In college, I earned my way by directing plays in community theaters; it was from this experience that I learned about directing. In the Red Cross war service, I taught a course and became a teacher. In New Guinea, as the field director on base, I delivered good news and bad news to servicepeople in the front lines—and in the process learned to be a social worker.

When the Ford Motor Company planned a big exhibition to introduce its dramatically new model car, I staged the first industrial show. I used my experience from that to teach a course to future producers of such shows. At the National Training Laboratories (NTL) in Bethel, Maine, where applied behavioral science was pioneered and the social invention of the T-group (the forerunner of sensitivity training, personal development, and organization development) was developed, I introduced "staging" to the presentation of theory and concepts in large meetings. For the 1950 White House Conference on Children and Youth, I created a mechanism that made it possible for six thousand people to have a discussion. Thanks to these experiences, I was then retained to design a number of large conferences, conventions, and sales meetings. It's as if the dodo in Lewis Carroll's *Alice's Adventures in Wonderland* was speaking to me and saying, "The best way to explain it is to do it."

Who Should Read This Book?

The driving force behind finally organizing the material and memories of my life into a book had to be its audience. Who would read the book? Who should? How could people benefit from it? What do I want the readers to take away from their efforts?

Those who read this book are value adders, facilitators, coaches. They are not the team on the field, or the actors on the stage, or the line managers. What they do is help development happen by creating concepts to describe and guide behavior, by designing mechanisms and interventions, by creating conditions for individuals and organizations to develop. The readers of this book—those who will directly benefit from it—are agents of change.

My hope is to change readers' understanding. That is no small task, especially given my sense that true learning is always transactional and is always a change process. After you learn something, you are different than before you learned it. In the process, some knowledge and experience and wisdom must be transferred.

Organization and Overview

The book is designed to be useful on a number of levels. Chapters can be read independently of each other, in order of the reader's interest. When read as a whole, the overall structure provides a mix of the chronology of my journey, major learnings and their applications to consulting and being an agent of change, and applications to larger fields of practice, including organization development, large systems change, consulting in the health field, and consulting to family businesses.

The book has three streams: my own story; the history of various fields (including human relations training, organization development, family business consulting, management in the health sector, and large systems change); and a time line from the fifties through the mid-nineties. Throughout, I articulate my principles of practice, my values and assumptions, and how they have affected my work.

The organization of the book is intended to embrace both the chronology of my journey through life and careers and major learnings and applications from my experiences. In Chapter One, I provide a brief autobiography and point out the major fields in which I have worked. I describe, in compressed form, the first thirty years of my life, the years before I started my applied behavioral science career in the summer of 1950 at NTL. Then I give an overview of the remainder of my second career—as a change agent, which is covered in more detail in later chapters. (My first was as a stage manager for theater productions!)

In Chapters Two through Five, I provide details on the developing fields, starting in Chapter Two with NTL and laboratory learning. In this chapter, I detail my experience and learnings in becoming a human relations trainer, as well as the effects of these learnings on my future work and career.

Chapter Three describes managing relationships, both personal and professional. I describe my discovery of the centrality of relationships as part of life and part of any change or consulting activity. I look at the interdependencies of personal and professional relationships and describe some of my significant mentors and friends and their impact on my life. I note my major learnings about the dilemmas of managing the tension between personal and professional relationships with clients or students; I touch on some of the methods I helped develop.

In Chapter Four, I reflect on how I became and learned how to be an organization consultant—my doing-learning pattern in action. Here I describe in detail the change model that I developed, used, and taught over the years. I look at the process of consulting and provide advice with all the benefit of my experience and the blessing of 20–20 hindsight.

Chapter Five is about organization development (OD) as a field and my roles in it. I review the naming of the field, the defining and codifying of it. I describe my realization of the need for professional training for practitioners and how I created the Program for Specialists in Organization Development (PSOD) at NTL in 1967, which then became the stimulus for a number of other degree and certificate programs.

Chapter Six reviews my experience in working both as a consultant and a leadership trainer in other countries and cultures, mainly in Europe and Latin America, beginning in the early sixties. I describe some early leadership training programs that used NTL methodologies and other techniques.

Chapter Seven describes my entry into academia and my learnings about the teaching-learning process. The development of conceptual models and tools and ways to apply designs from the classroom to professional development training are included as well. In this chapter, I address my role as a teacher and some of the models and tools I developed to help people, whether in school or on the job, to be students and learners. I reflect on my twenty-one years on the faculty at the Sloan School at MIT (Massachusetts Institute of Technology), some of the more innovative activities I conducted, and some learnings from the experience that I then applied to professional and management training.

Chapter Eight looks at large system change. I describe a number of massive change efforts using educational interventions in countries from Denmark to the United States, with people whose roles ranged from CEO to missionary. I examine a significant application of my learnings and change skills in a countrywide change program in Columbia and in other venues such as hospitals and medical schools.

In Chapter Nine, I discuss consulting to family businesses, a long-time concern of mine that has, over time, become a field in its own right and a major part of my practice. The chapter is really a case study of the development of a field from an idea in my head to a professional network with an association, the Family Firm Institute (FFI), with over a thousand members. I also review how family businesses became a significant part of management education and university-industry collaborations.

In Chapter Ten, I discuss adding value, senior style: my experience of trying to find ways of making a useful contribution and leading a meaningful work life after I was no longer "active" in my field—a transition that is a challenge to many.

In the final chapter of the book, Chapter Eleven, I predict the future of the various fields in which I have been involved. I outline my educated guess as to what will evolve in organizational development and how practitioners might best prepare now for that future. I also look to the future of large system change and helping the leadership of family businesses. I offer some advice, based on my experience and experiencing, to those consultants, change agents, teachers, counselors, and coaches who, today and tomorrow, are making change happen in the world and making the world a better place through the application of their skills as agents of change.

Throughout the chapters, I review my major writings, conceptual models, and tools that I have designed for use in facilitating and managing change and complexity. Some of the models and tools are described in more detail in the Resources section.

Acknowledgments

This book would not have been what it is without the help and guidance of four people in particular. Special thanks go to Bill Hicks, now publisher of the New Lexington Press, an imprint of Jossey-Bass, who helped make it happen; to Cedric Crocker, senior editor of the business and management series at Jossey-Bass, who played midwife in the development of the last three versions; to Janet Hunter, freelance developmental editor, whose editorial skills and understanding of what I was trying to say have made this book readable; and to Sonia Millett, who typed and retyped and retyped yet again various versions of the manuscript.

Shared Wisdom

As I have mentioned, this book is my attempt to transfer my learnings and experience to readers. I hope that those readers will, in turn, add their own experience and learnings to enrich the fields of practice the book describes. It is my firm belief that no one can truly copyright an idea. Nor, if we are to continue to change and improve, should this be possible. Many of the ideas in this book first evolved from my exposure to others' experience and wisdom—that of clients and students alike. It is my hope that the book's readers will keep the transfer process alive and well in the years ahead.

New York City   Dick Beckhard
July 1997

The Author

Dick Beckhard has been involved with the management of change for more years than he cares to describe. As one of the founders of the field of organization development (OD), he helped define it as an area of study and practice.

Beckhard has been a consultant with chief executives, boards, and senior managers of organizations in both the private and public sectors. Some of his long-time clients included Proctor & Gamble and Imperial Chemical Industries. He was professor of organization behavior and management at the Sloan School of Management, Massachusetts Institute of Technology, from 1963 to 1984.

Beckhard has authored, coauthored, and coedited many books, including *Organization Development Strategies* (1969), *Organization Transitions* (1977, 2nd ed. 1987), *Changing the Essence* (1993), *Organization of the Future* (1996), and *Leader of the Future* (1996). He has written numerous articles in the field of change management.

Beckhard has been adjunct professor at Case Western University, London Graduate School of Business, Teachers College at Columbia University, and Pepperdine University. He provides large systems consulting for chief executive officers, coaches professional management consultants, and speaks at workshops and seminars. Since 1968 Beckhard has been coeditor of the Addison Wesley OD Series. He serves on the advisory board of the Peter F. Drucker Foundation for Nonprofit Management and is an active member of the Family Firm Institute and the Office of Public Management.

1

The First Thirty Years
A Brief Biography

The story of my second career—my journey and learnings as an agent of change—parallels a series of histories in the field: the history of human relations training, of organization development, of managing change, of consulting to large complex systems, of the consulting process, of using educational interventions as a strategy for large systems change, of the field of family business consulting, and of professional development programs for organization and organization development consultants. But to fully understand my role in these fields and what I have learned and shared during the forty-nine years of this journey, to understand my process, consulting style, values, and assumptions, as well as my contributions to applied behavioral science in a number of settings, we need to go further back—back to my first career and its underpinnings.

I joined the world in April 1918, in Whitestone Queens, New York City. My father, who was a pioneer in the development of the outboard motor, had a marina in Flushing, New York, where he sold outboards. He also built racing boats and had several drivers who drove his boats in the races.

In the twenties, my life was totally protected. My grandfather was a millionaire investment banker. My father's business was successful. In the summers Dad would be involved in the racing season, both as a competitor-owner and as a judge of various races. My mother and I would follow him from regatta to regatta in the early summers. In late June we would go up to "camp," our cabin in Maine on Lake Kezar, which Dad had built in 1903 when he was in college at Harvard.

Life was idyllic and easy. I went to public schools in the winter and enjoyed camp life in the summers. I was the only grandson in my family and was pampered and spoiled by my grandfather, as well as my parents. I performed one useful role in life during that time. When my father and his colleagues were trying out new types of outboards to see how they would work in different types of boats, I came in handy. I was about the same size and weight as a sandbag, and a lot easier to move.

In 1928, I had bronchial pneumonia, and the doctor recommended that we go to Florida for my recovery for a few weeks. My sister, who was born when I was five and had always been frail—the family story was that as a baby she fit into a shoe box—would also benefit from spending part of the winter in the South.

Dad rented a small apartment in the little town of Gulfport, a suburb of St. Petersburg. We had a fine stay there, I recovered, and my father fell in love with the place. My parents decided we would come down for the whole winter the following year, 1929. My sister and I would go to school in St. Petersburg. So the following year we drove down to Gulfport in my grandfather's Pierce Arrow limo with William, his long-time chauffeur, at the wheel.

Three days after we arrived, the stock market crashed. The next day, my father's business burned up. We were suddenly poor.

My father used some of the $2,000 in his pocket to send William and the car back to New York. He bought a little house near the water (where he could keep a boat) for $1,200. That became my home for the next six years and my parents' home until they both died.

I went to junior high school and high school in St. Petersburg. We lived the small town life—in a small town culture. The early picture of a beautiful town, which my parents had in 1928, was replaced by the reality of a small, conservative, almost red-neck community, where African Americans (*not* the term in use at the time) had to be off the street at five o'clock.

Having very little money, we scraped through the Depression. My dad built a dock nine hundred feet into the bay over the sandbar. The local fishermen used it, and in return we had plenty of fish. I still can't look at a pompano.

My first entrepreneurial venture was selling *The Saturday Evening Post*. The magazine's strategy was to have children sell the magazines on the streets. You bought some copies, at least ten, for two cents apiece and sold them at five cents. The company gave you a canvas bag to carry ten copies. When you sold them, you picked up more at your house and went out again.

My "market" was the elderly tourists at the beach and park area five blocks from our house. A few days before my first Thursday delivery day, I broke my collarbone diving into shallow water in a pond at a Boy Scout retreat. My arm was in a sling, and I could barely carry the bag of magazines. The bag almost touched the ground (I've always been very short). My father drove me down to the beach, and I staggered out with my magazines. When I appeared on the beach sidewalk, weaving under this load, I was an instant hit. Little old ladies rushed to buy my magazines. Wives told their husbands to buy a magazine from the poor little kid. I sold my ten copies in fifteen minutes and rushed back for more. In all, I sold forty copies that day.

The distributor was pleased with my performance. I realized I had a "business opportunity." So every Thursday throughout the tourist season, I would put on my sling, get a ride to the beach, and sell my magazines. I soon became top salesman in my district. I won a couple of prizes, which I never put on the mantelpiece.

Succumbing to the Theater Bug

When I was twelve, my uncle, a theatrical producer, had a summer theater in Greenwich, Connecticut, where he presented a different play each week. One week he was trying out a play that he'd written in which the heroine was a piano teacher. In the opening scene of the second act, she was giving a piano lesson to a little "brat." My uncle found it difficult to cast the brat part, so he turned to the original model: me. (He'd seen and heard me taking a piano lesson.)

Although that play flopped, during the same season he tried out a play called "Another Language" that was a hit. At the end of the summer season he moved it to Broadway where it was a smash success, and it ran for over a year. From that experience in the summer of 1931, I knew that the theater was my destiny.

One summer during high school, I stage-managed a season of plays, again for my uncle, in Highland, New York. The theater critic at the *St. Petersburg Times* had to take a leave, and the editor allowed me to fill in for a few weeks. The *Times* then hired me to be the Gulfport correspondent. I was paid by the inch/line. I became a cub reporter, working the police beat with the real reporters. My hours were 5 P.M. to midnight or so. I would get home at 1 A.M., sleep for a few hours, catch the bus for school at 7:30, come home for early supper, and head back to the paper. I thrived on it.

Yet I never liked St. Petersburg. The culture of the area was Byzantine. Even so, high school was fun. I acted in and directed plays, sang in the chorus, and had a good social life.

Our economic condition was marginal; the only income was some interest from what was left of my father's portfolio of stocks. I realized that I would have to earn enough to support myself and to contribute significantly to my family. The *Times* provided some income. As I approached high school graduation, it became painfully obvious that my choices of places to obtain an affordable higher education were very limited. There was one option—St. Petersburg Community College—which I did not want to take.

At that time, my uncle and aunt were both working in Hollywood, she as an actress and he as a writer-director. They invited me to spend the summer with them in Los Angeles. We found the train

fare, and I left, never to come back except to visit. During that summer I met Everett Dean Martin at a guest ranch where my uncle
and aunt spent some weekends. He was on his way to join the faculty of Scripps, a women's college that was one of three schools
making up the Claremont Colleges. I knew I had to take his classes.
That was only possible if I was at Pomona College, the sister college to Scripps. It was only three days before the start of the term,
but Dr. Dean Martin got an appointment for me with the admis-
sions director. With no credentials, no transcript, no money—only
an Honorary Scholastic Society key from high school—I would
need a scholarship and a job. I told the director I desperately wanted
to attend Pomona.

The director was taken with my "brashness." He said that
although no scholarships remained, he could arrange a grant-in-aid
(a student loan) for my tuition. The following Monday I attended
freshman orientation at Pomona. I had to pay for my food and housing. All the campus jobs were taken for the first semester. The only
job he knew about was washing pots and pans at the local restaurant. I took the job. But I was working my way through and providing major support for my parents, so I needed more work. I
started a cleaning and laundry pickup service. Students left their
clothes in my room; I sent them to the laundry; on return I
delivered the clothes to the students, who paid me. And I got a
commission from the laundry. I also got a National Youth Administration grant (an FDR Depression program) that allowed me to
become assistant director in the theater department. In later years
at Pomona, I augmented my income by directing plays at Little
Theaters in the area.

My years at Pomona College were full and fun. In addition to
my drama work, I sang in the Pomona Glee Club, then the top club
in the nation. In the summers I worked as stage manager in my
uncle's theater in Santa Barbara. After college I stage-managed a
play, "The Male Animal," to which my uncle had the rights. We
toured the play in California, and it was a hit.

My uncle could not afford to keep the rights, so the authors, James Turner and Elliott Nugent, sold them to Herman Shumlin, a successful Broadway producer. I tried to get the stage manager's job in the New York production, but it was filled. One Tuesday I telegraphed the theater manager, whom I knew, asking if they would at least interview me for the assistant's job since I knew the play. Rehearsals were starting the next Monday so I would have to be there on Saturday to have any chance of getting the job. They told me that if I could get to New York by Saturday, they would see me. I borrowed the train fare, ate bananas for the five-day trip, arrived in New York, and got the assistant's job.

During rehearsals the stage manager, who was a full-time writer and a friend of the producer but who had no stage managing experience, told the producer the job was too hard for him. He suggested that we switch positions. That was the start of my Broadway career.

I was draft-deferred at the start of World War II because I was supporting my parents. When I was no longer deferrable, I was drafted. After a series of draft board physical exam papers were lost, I finally went to an induction center for my physical exam—and was rejected because of a hernia. I was classified 4F, that is, not available for induction for physical reasons.

I had been a founder and one of the operators of the Stage Door Canteen, a night club for servicemen run by the American Theatre Wing, Broadway's contribution to the war effort. While at the canteen, I made an arrangement with the local Red Cross Services to the Armed Forces organization so that Red Cross workers who were waiting to leave the Port of New York for their overseas assignments could "work" at the club as hostesses. This meant bending the Red Cross rule that workers must always be in uniform.

The Red Cross officials had known of my pre-induction status. They tried to recruit me for service with them, but I was too caught up in the system to be able to do anything about it. When I was made 4F, I went directly from the induction center to the Red Cross headquarters and told them I was ready to join them.

Doing and Learning

It was at the Red Cross that my pattern of doing and learning started. The Red Cross staff were all professional social or recreation workers. I was neither. The Red Cross in Washington was starting a new four-week training program for people who would be in leadership roles overseas in the hospitals, recreation clubs, and field canteens. They needed someone to teach the drama and music course in the program. I had never taught anything in my life.

I knew that I would have to take a physical after six months, and if I flunked it I couldn't go into the field overseas, which was what I wanted to do. I negotiated that I would teach the course, provided that I was on a ship before six months (when I'd have to have the physical exam). Amazingly they agreed. They were desperate for faculty.

I started teaching, knowing nothing about curricula or course plans. For the drama material I had the students write and act in skits and mini-plays (as training for doing shows with the GIs). For the music, the main need was to conduct sing-alongs at camps and clubs. The training? I would stand up front and sing a song from "Oklahoma," the hit musical. I would sing, "Oh, What a Beautiful Morning," or "Surrey with the Fringe on Top." After one verse I'd ask the class to sing with me. I would then have students come up and lead the singing. My course was a great success.

One of the students in the first four-week class (a new class started every two weeks) was Alethea (we all called her Lee) Hanson, a social worker, who was an executive in the national office of the Girl Scouts. She liked my singing. We met, fell in love, and decided to marry. For the next three months I commuted to New York, where she was waiting to be shipped somewhere. I managed to get her off the roster. She came to Washington to join the faculty; we married on September 11, 1943 (a happy marriage that would last until her death thirty-two years later).

On December 26th we both left the States—she for Europe, I for New Guinea. My first assignment was as a recreation worker in

Milne Bay, building a thatched hut for a program. Later I was promoted to field director—the social work job of working with the GIs (about which I knew nothing). Six months later, I was made area director. My area included New Guinea and the Admiralty Islands, a ten-thousand-mile area. This was a top management job in which I was responsible for sixteen hundred staff members and a budget of $6 million. Somebody must have read a wrong bio. The only management I'd ever done was stage managing. I had to learn the whole management process fast. I learned, often quite literally, "on the wing," as I flew from base to base on the Air Force mail plane. These two years were full of "doing and learning," in everything from the duties of a recreation director to working as the Red Cross representative on a task force planning an invasion of Japan.

Beginning a Transition

In 1946 I returned to the theater. I directed some summer plays and in 1947 was production manager for Lillian Hellman's play, "Another Part of the Forest." That was the last of my work in productions on Broadway. When the play closed, I had no immediate prospects for another job.

I began for the first time to question whether my future was in stage managing and directing. I knew that although I was an effective director of plays that had already been produced, I was less effective in bringing a new play to the stage. I knew also that I would never be a Joshua Logan or George Abbott, the top directors at that time. I had, since I was fourteen, realized that I had to depend on my own wits and resources to achieve anything. Working in the theater was a high-risk business. I had managed to survive and find enough work to make a living, but this type of world had no assured future for me. Lee was working and we lived on her salary—not a satisfying condition.

Fate and opportunity intervened. The American Theatre Wing created a professional school for theater people who had been in the service and were now returning to their professions. This came at a time when there were fewer shows on Broadway and less activity in dance and music for people seeking work. The leadership of the Theatre Wing thought that a professional school, supported by the GI Bill, would provide an alternative to total unemployment. They set up three schools: theater, music and dance, and radio-TV.

I was asked to put together a curriculum for the theater school and to teach in it. This meant some income and a steady job, for which I was more than ready. I had no formal experience in setting up a program, but I did it and tried to learn as I went. I established a course in theater management for regional theaters. From this I became a consultant to a number of community theaters.

A company asked me to stage a sales meeting, which I did and subsequently got some other offers to stage meetings. A magazine, *Sales Meetings*, was entering its third year of publication. Its publisher had somehow heard of my work; he asked me to be a contributing editor and to write about staging meetings. I had never written a column, but fate decreed that I should. I wrote, learning as I went how to write a column.

The next big break came in 1947. The Ford Motor Company was bringing out a radically different kind of car the following year, and they needed to make the public aware of it. There was little TV in those days. They decided to put on a big industrial show, where dealers from all over and the public in New York could be exposed to the new cars. Ford rented the whole ballroom floor of the Waldorf-Astoria for a week and contracted with Walter Dorwin Teague, a top industrial designer, to design a series of exhibits. Ford wanted six thousand people an hour to move through the exhibition and needed some staging to keep the traffic flowing. Teague contacted a friend of mine, Phil Barber, who then suggested that I be hired to produce the entertainment. I put together a series of presentations that would move people. With an unlimited budget, I hired the Paul Whiteman Band to provide music and actors to work with the displays. I developed a series of mini-shows that one could watch and still keep moving. I designed a flow plan so that the audience was pulled along from exhibit to exhibit. It was a massive undertaking. Much to everyone's amazement, it worked well.

For me, there were two major by-products of this experience, one immediate and one longer term. The Ford special projects expert, Crosby Kelly, who produced the show, was hired to be the executive director of a "World's Fair," a railroad fair to be held on the Chicago waterfront in 1950. Kelly hired me to put together the entertainment that would be in the fair. The second by-product was that I was now recognized as an expert in staging and a new field of practice—industrial shows—opened to me.

I conducted a course on industrial shows at the Theatre Wing School, wrote a chapter on industrial shows in a theater publication, and became an instant expert in industrial shows. In the process, I had developed systems of communication for control of traffic flow. I had learned how to use theater techniques to stimulate interest in a product quickly. I then took those learnings and applied them to the staging of a number of sales meetings and large conferences. First among them, the Girl Scouts of America, retained me to stage the general sessions at its next triennial conference. This was to be attended by eight hundred or so delegates from councils all over the United States. I knew the organization, in part because my wife was a Girl Scout executive, and I knew about staging.

I used my theater and industrial show experience to make the plenary sessions interesting. We needed some way for small groups to discuss issues in the general meetings. The technique of buzz groups (people in a large room talking to each other in groups of six to eight) had just been invented. I designed a system for holding such discussions, as well as a method in which, by using microphones in the aisles, delegates could discuss pros and cons of any issue in an orderly manner, with the meeting chair in control. Over the years, I refined this methodology, which is still used today in large meetings. My learnings from this experience were to be very important to me throughout the years, particularly as I began the transition into the next phase of my career.

Starting Over: A New Career

It was my work in staging meetings (and my friend Phil Barber) that brought me to the attention of Ron Lippitt and Lee Bradford, two of the three founders of the National Training Laboratories. And it was because of them that, as described in the next chapter, I spent a momentous summer commuting between the Chicago Fair and the NTL session in Bethel, Maine. I would leave the Chicago Fair on Sunday evenings in a red, open Cadillac, be driven to Midway Airport, catch a DC-3 for the two-hour flight to New York. After a quick dinner at LaGuardia Airport, I would fly to Portland, Maine, and then I would drive to Bethel. On Friday afternoon I would reverse the process.

That summer in Bethel changed my life, helped me to become aware of and articulate my values and beliefs, and drove me into my second career, which is currently forty-seven years old. Since that summer of 1950, my career has had one or two major themes in each decade, which are explained in more detail in the rest of the book. The major theme in the fifties was learning: learning to become a human relations trainer and a consultant, with corollary learnings about consulting, large systems, and family businesses. The major themes in the sixties were organization development, becoming an international consultant, and joining academia. A minor theme was expanding professional education. In the seventies, in addition to teaching and consulting, a major theme was working in the health field. Here I could apply management theory and practice to medical education. In the eighties, a major theme was developing the field of family business consulting. I also retired from the university and began the process, continued in the nineties, of winding down my consulting work and learning to add value as a "retired" professional.

In the time frame of this book, I have written and seen published seven books, chapters in other books, numerous journal and magazine articles, speeches, videos, and training films. The books are listed below; books, articles, speeches, and films are listed in Resource A. The models and tools I have developed throughout my career are described in later chapters. Supporting materials that may be of use are included in the Resources section.

- *Blueprint for Summer Theatre*, published by John Richard Press, 1948.
- *How to Plan and Conduct Workshops and Conferences*, published by the Association Press, 1956.
- *The Fact-Finding Conference*, coauthored with Warren Schmidt and published by the Adult Education Association, 1956.
- *Organization Development: Strategies and Models*, published as part of the Addison-Wesley organization development series in 1969. This was the second-biggest seller in the series, after Edgar Schein's *Process Consultation*.
- *Organization Transitions: Managing Complex Change*, coauthored with Reuben Harris and published in 1977 for the same series. Our revised edition was published in 1987.
- *The View from Shangri-La—Seventy Summers on Lake Kezar*. Privately published in 1991, this is my book about life in Maine.
- *Changing the Essence: The Art of Creating and Leading Fundamental Change in Organizations*, coauthored with Wendy Pritchard, published by Jossey-Bass, 1992.

When I attended my first NTL workshop, it was to *do* the general sessions. Because I was there, I joined a learning group and became exposed to the laboratory method of learning. At the time, I considered it just an interesting experience. It was only afterward, when I reflected on the impact of the experience on my life, that I began to see the learning method as a metaphor for my own life. The laboratory method was to produce behavior, analyze the behavior, generalize from the analysis, look at applications of the generalizations, and produce some more behavior. The activity was a form of action research; group participants were both the subjects and the researchers. As my career progressed and my self-awareness and group skills increased, the metaphor became a major force in my understanding of what I was doing and learning in the laboratory of my life. And that is reflected in the organization of this book.

2

A Transition
Becoming a Human Relations Trainer

In the spring of 1950, I had a visit from Ronald Lippitt and Leland Bradford, two of the three founders of NTL (the third was Kenneth Benne). Bradford was the director of the Adult Education Division of the National Education Association. NTL had been set up as a subset of the division; Bradford was named its director. Lippitt was an associate of Kurt Lewin, the founder of group dynamics, and was then head of the Research Center for Group Dynamics at the University of Michigan. Lippitt, whose wife was a faculty member of the Psychodrama Institute in Beacon, New York, wanted to know if the technique of role playing (an offshoot of psychodrama, a therapy in which people play roles in order to understand motivation or interpersonal dynamics) would be effective on television, the new medium, for training purposes (rather than as therapy). I had no idea but agreed to do a test. We rented a laboratory room with one-way glass at Teachers College, Columbia. I recruited a group and designed some training exercises using role playing. Lippitt and Barber recruited an "audience" who would watch the group through the one-way glass. Lippitt would study the audience reactions.

The results of our experiment were negative for applications to TV but positive for me: I got to know Ron Lippitt, a giant in his field. He asked me if I would be interested in attending the forthcoming summer session of NTL to study the general sessions. He thought that if I could watch them, I could come up with a way of making this important part of the program more effective.

In the general sessions, which were theory presentations, theory and concepts were presented by the staff to help the participants understand group dynamics and interpersonal relationships. The session content was excellent but the presentations were often dull and uninteresting. Lippitt and Bradford felt that the communication could be improved if the staging were more creative. Knowing of my theater background, they asked me to do this study. As a quid pro quo, they offered me a scholarship to attend the sessions and join a T-group.

The T-group was an unstructured group, with no formal structure, agenda, or leadership pattern. The participants had to develop a structure, an agenda, a method of making decisions, and a leadership system. This concept, a major social invention, had been developed in the summer of 1947 at the first program of the National Training Laboratories. It was based on the behavioral method. The "theory" behind it was premised on the idea that if a group of individuals find themselves totally without structure, they must fall back on their basic styles of handling ambiguity. The goal of the training was to learn about *process*—the dynamics of what goes on while a group is "working" on a subject. Therefore, the *process* became the *content* of the discussion. To achieve this, the staff created a theory of "Laboratory Learning," in which the participants were simultaneously acting in the groups and being in them as "researchers," looking at what was going on in the action.

My Entry into the World of Laboratory Learning

I first attended the program in the summer of 1950, the fourth year of the programs, held in Bethel, Maine. This particular year, they were trying an experiment. The population was divided into six groups: Four of them were the unstructured T-group; two were highly structured groups with structured exercises, looking at power,

leadership, communications, and related topics. Al Zander and Irv-
ing Knickerbocker had used these structured groups in their research
on group dynamics at the University of Michigan in the late 1940s.

I had flown in Sunday night from Chicago, so I missed the opening general session. After breakfast on Monday I showed up for my
T-group meeting. I had been told by some folks that this would be
a powerful experience—everyone at breakfast was both nervous and
expectant. There were sixteen people in my group. The leader
(Zander) broke us into four groups and gave us the tasks of getting
to know each other and of sharing some areas of behavior that we
wanted to improve with our three colleagues. This wasn't frighten-
ing at all; in fact, it was quite comfortable. Zander went on to
explain some of the dynamics of groups and that we would be learning about decision making, power, leadership, and so forth. Sounded
great. We had a fine morning, and I looked forward to the next
group session scheduled for the following morning.

In the afternoon the program called for "social action groups."
The founders of NTL believed that the only counterpoint to the
repressive McCarthy tactics of the time would be if the volunteer
and social sectors rose up in protest. The founders were committed
to working with organization leaders in the social sector to improve
their social action skills. (This position was rarely discussed in the
literature about NTL, but it was a strong force in driving the
program.)

For this aspect of the program, the community had again been
divided into several groups, each relatively homogeneous, with people of like backgrounds (often teams from the same agency) assigned
to a group. In the assignment process, the staff had a problem. There
were a number of delegates, as they called the participants, who
were not connected with any social action group. A decision was
made to create one hybrid group, and it was a real mishmash. It
included a major in the army, two admirals from the navy, a
destroyer commander, a minister, a psychoanalyst, two women volunteers from the Denver Adult Education Council, and me, from

the theater. We were doomed from the start, but what an experience! I knew nothing about the program. Nor did I know then that the staff had drawn straws to determine the trainer. As we sat down and wrote our names on table cards, I saw that Lee Bradford, whom I had met in New York, was the loser and was to be our leader. I felt comfortable and secure.

We sat there, and Lee didn't say anything. There were no opening remarks. This didn't fit the articulate man I had met in New York, but I figured that was what laboratory learning was about. After a minute, a man and two young women came in and sat down in the front of the room. The women took out shorthand pads and began to write. The man held up a picture of a group sitting around a table, with one man leaving the room. He said, "You have the following task. As a group you are to decide what is going on, what caused it, and what is going to happen next. You have fifteen minutes."

There followed a dead silence. I looked at Lee. He was playing with a golf tee. After an unbearable time, the army major jumped up, rushed to the blackboard, drew some vertical lines, and said, "We've got to get going. Let's separate what went before, now, and the future. Let's start with the picture. Who's got an idea?"

There was dead silence from the group. After what seemed to be twenty minutes but was probably two, I couldn't stand it any longer. I thought the army major, the one person who'd volunteered to do the assigned task, was treated rudely by the group. I felt that the researcher had asked a straightforward question, so I proceeded to talk through a one-act play describing the situation and what was going on with each of the characters.

Again dead silence. Finally the man and two women left. We again fell into silence. Lee did nothing, still made no opening remarks. From that we started the usual T-group experience: we addressed questions such as, What will we do? How will we make decisions? Who should be leader?

Our group was so fractured that we could not do anything. It took us four days of meetings to decide on a process to elect one of our members to be a representative at the community council that met after class every afternoon to monitor how things were going in the community. When we finally did elect a person, after three straw votes (How would we think everyone would vote if we voted now?), we elected the quietest person—one of the women from Denver. She started to thank us for our confidence, and we jumped all over her. She went to the council meeting in tears.

By the end of the meeting we had more psychologists and psychiatrists sitting in the windows studying us than we had group members. As I learned later, the researchers who came into the room were doing a Thematic Apperception Test (rather like a group Rorschach) as part of a research project run by Murray Horowitz, a faculty member at the Institute for Social Research at the University of Michigan. They repeated the test at the end of the program with our group and the five other groups. The members of our group said, "Let Dick do it." And they all left the room. Our group behavior was so aberrant that our group's data were scrapped from the research.

Learning for a Transition

Although I didn't completely realize it at the time, I had undergone a profound experience. Those three weeks changed my life. The most profound effect of my first experience with NTL laboratory training was a dramatic increase in self-awareness.

I had gone through life pretty much as a loner. In the theater I was a director. In the Red Cross I was a manager. In the post-war years I was a dean and an agency executive. In these worlds, who I was was defined by what I did. I was a director of theatrical and dramatic events, whether a Broadway play, or a sales meeting, or a convention, or a pageant. But in the group at NTL, none of my history mattered a bit. I was just a person; my roles or identities were irrelevant. People reacted to me and let me know their reactions. The training group forced me to think about myself as a person—my "personality"—how I related to others, mostly in a support or helping capacity, but one of high influence.

It also helped me think about my values and beliefs. What drove me? What did I think was important to keep in my life? I had never experienced anything like this before. It was an incredible experience and one that sharpened my awareness of my lack of clarity about my next career steps. I knew that I was transitioning out of the theater world, but I had no idea what I was transitioning into. At the end of the session, Lee Bradford lit a fire under my transition by asking me to come back the next summer (1951) to manage the general sessions program. I was delighted. The prospect ensured that I could spend the summer in Maine, at my cabin twenty miles away, with paid employment for at least six weeks. But what of the rest of the year?

I have long believed and stated that when a major organizational change is needed and planned, you cannot move from condition A to condition B without going through a transition state. A metaphor I have often used is that of shifting gears in your automobile: you shouldn't move from one gear to another without going through neutral. The same is true for any kind of change. Regardless of the clarity of the goal, a transition state—a state in which you are shedding old behavior and attitudes before bringing in the new condition—is needed to get there.

The NTL experience had changed my thinking and attitudes about myself and my relationships. I had learned a lot about groups from the staff presentations and the group experience, about learning, about change, but I had no idea what to do with the knowledge. I knew that my career in the theater and related activities was finished. The Chicago Fair closed; my contract expired. I was now without a job, with no foreseeable source of income and not the remotest idea what I wanted to do with my life. I had saved a little money from my salary from the fair. My wife and I decided to go away for a couple of weeks and think about where I was, without knowing where I was going. She was smart enough to realize I needed to be "in neutral" for a while. We rented a small apartment in a bed and breakfast in Bermuda.

We looked at what I had done, what skills I had developed: directing, staging large meetings, and from NTL, some knowledge about small group workings. There had been a heavy emphasis on research during the workshop, with daily presentations by researchers. We, the participants, were used as subjects in a number of experiments, which we hated.

I could not see any connection between the information we were getting and any of my own prior experience. I found it difficult to reconcile the theory with the real-life situations I had seen. What was the connection between research on bomber crews as teams in the war and building work teams in a factory? What was the connection between the finding that a group setting provided an optimum situation for individual learning and commitment to action, and the issue in organizations of getting salesmen committed to action on organization goals? Was there an alternative to the "give 'em hell" inspirational sales meetings? My wife, bless her heart, could see a connection. She pointed out that small groups usually functioned in meetings. I had some expertise in staging large meetings. Now I had some knowledge of small groups. I could take advantage of the discrepancy between the academic jargon on research findings and the practical problems I had heard discussed in meetings I had staged. One of the very common complaints I had heard was about the terrible waste of time in meetings of all kinds. There were too many meetings, they took too long, they were inefficient and boring, and they kept people from doing "real work." Yet, much of the organization's work—communications, planning, monitoring—needed to be in some group setting.

As I thought about the presentations on theories about effective group functioning and about the ways meetings were actually conducted, I realized there was little connection between the two. The knowledge and understandings that were being discovered were not being translated or applied to managers or leaders in organizations.

A light flashed. Perhaps what was needed was a "bridge" between the two worlds—someone who understood the principles and theory and who could translate and help apply them to the communications problems and challenges facing managers. Would my limited exposure to the theory and practice of face-to-face group workings make it possible for me to play that bridging role? I had always been a catalyst. Perhaps by applying what I knew about the dynamics of groups—the communication-participation pattern, hidden agendas, goals, leadership—I could provide the necessary bridge and improve meetings. I couldn't find any consulting firm that specialized in this arena. I saw both a need and a niche. I would become a meetings consultant and perhaps find a role helping managers improve the effectiveness of their meetings. As a contributing editor of *Sales Meetings Magazine*, I had already committed to writing some articles on sales meetings. Maybe I could find some methods for helping managers have ways of making all their meetings more effective.

I had $1,900 to my name, the residue of my savings from the Red Cross work in the war. My wife had a job. We had a house. My friend Phil Barber offered to give me a small office in his suite. I went to the license bureau and registered as doing business as Conference Counselors. The staff was me. I got my certificate and I was "in business." Never mind that I had no money and no clients. I shared the widely held perception that defining oneself as a consultant in something was a way of describing that you were an expert in that something. I was fortunate that I soon had an opportunity to test my expertise.

The White House Conference

Every ten years a White House Conference on Children and Youth was convened in Washington. In preparation for the conference, state conferences were held the preceding year. The purpose of the project was to find the areas of consensus around public policy on youth affairs, in order to provide guidance to the agencies charged with creating and implementing national policy.

Mel Glasser, a social work executive, was the director. Mel had been best man at my hastily arranged wartime wedding, mainly because he had been available that Saturday afternoon when no other friends were. He had hired Gordon Lippitt, then a senior staff member of NTL, to be program director. I saw the opportunity and contacted Glasser to offer my services to help design the plenary meetings.

He was pleased with my offer. He told me that my meetings management and design experience could make a contribution. Unfortunately, he was already over budget and would not be able to pay me. He bought me lunch. Afterward, I got on the train back from Washington to New York. As we were approaching Philadelphia, I realized, "Dick, you are a fool! This is a fantastic opportunity!" This being long before cellular telephones, or even pay telephones on trains, I got off the train at Philadelphia and called him in Washington. I told him I would pay him for the chance to contribute. He said he could cover expenses. I was appointed consultant to the program director.

The logistics issues of the conference were formidable. Everything I had learned and done I was able to put to use. There were six thousand people trying to develop recommendations that would guide federal and state policies on children for the next ten years. Almost all the conference time was in plenary sessions.

There was a major conflict, somewhat church-driven, about whether private schools, such as Catholic schools, could receive support from government. The issue, separation of church and state, provoked high conflict and is still very much alive today. Then, the sides were so polarized that people almost came to blows over it. The findings and recommendations would have to be made in one two-hour plenary meeting. To have any kind of quality discussion was a daunting challenge. Mel Glasser and Gordon Lippitt needed to find a way for these issues to be discussed in some orderly way. They asked me to help them with the design of the final session.

I devised a system, based in part on my experience in handling large conventions. I drafted a design in which issues could be addressed and debated in an open meeting, applied some techniques from political conventions, devised some ways of caucusing during a debate, and consulted and guided the meeting chairs on the management of the process.

We placed microphones about fifty feet apart in both of the main aisles in the auditorium, as in political conventions. We created placards with station numbers on them and painted them on two sides: one side said "For"; the other side said "Against." Attendants would hold these placards. Delegates who wanted to speak would come to the microphone. The attendant would ask whether they were for or against the current question and would turn their placards to face the stage with the appropriate word visible so that the chair of the meeting could see it. The chair would then set the ground rules. He would recognize pros and cons alternately and would try to recognize stations in different parts of the room. We tried the scheme in some of the early sessions and it worked quite well. I installed a walkie-talkie communication system so that attendants at the mikes could hear me relay the instructions and other information.

The final session had to produce the recommendations that would go forward to the relevant agencies. After the heated discussions of the first days, the atmosphere was charged. People arrived as early as two hours before the meeting to line up at microphones. The meeting started and the chairman worked the system. It became apparent after an hour that the delegates were not going to arrive at any closure or consensus in one more hour. As people shouted, "We must continue this debate," the director and the leadership hastily convened a conference.

The two speakers who were to address the afternoon closing session were Walter Reuther, who as president of the United Auto Workers was known for his liberal thinking and inspiring speeches, and Kathryn Lenroot, the director of the Children's Bureau Agency (which sponsored the conference) and the person who would manage the carrying out of the recommendations. Glasser and the chairman consulted them. The speakers agreed that continuing the debate was much more important than their planned closing speeches.

The chairman then came to the podium microphone and acknowledged the overwhelming need of the delegates to continue. He told them that the speakers had graciously agreed not to speak. He announced that there would be a one-hour break and the meeting would continue until five o'clock, thus adding three more hours for discussion. The six thousand people in attendance rearranged their travel plans, grabbed a sandwich or ate a bag lunch, and came back to the meeting. They did develop recommendations. It was an incredible experience for all. The participants had an open discussion in plenary (no buzz groups) session through the process I had devised. People who spoke at the mikes were usually representatives of a delegation; they spoke for constituencies. It was democracy at work through a giant town meeting.

At the brief closing ceremony, Mel Glasser was kind enough to acknowledge my contribution to the process. Afterward, as I was trying to cool down from the excitement and euphoria of the moment, Constance Roach came up to me. She was the head of the cultural department in the state department's United States Commission for UNESCO. She had heard of me: my friend, Phil Barber, had mentioned my name and my work at the Ford meeting in 1947. She told me that the first UNESCO conference in the United

States was scheduled to be held at Hunter College in New York. Would I be interested in becoming a consultant to the commission and function as conference manager?

Moving into Laboratory Learning

From the condition of complete ambiguity six months earlier, I now had a project that would employ me for at least a year at a respectable salary. I arranged my work with the UNESCO commission so that I could participate in a three-week NTL program at Bethel. I was committed to continuing my personal learning journey, to continuing my exposure to laboratory learning, and to becoming a professional trainer. I now had the beginnings of a new identity. I was managing a large project. My business name of Conference Planners wasn't too far off the mark. I could take Lee Bradford up on his offer to join the staff and become an apprentice human relations trainer.

The 1950 experience had been a structured T-group and a social action group that didn't provide any social action but that functioned like a T-group, without the cognitive support to the experience. Now I could participate in a regular T-group—the real thing. Jack Glidwell was my trainer in what was quite a learning experience for me.

Lee Bradford was a wonderful support. In 1951 he let me join the afternoon faculty in conducting skill practice sessions. I learned how to do that. In my third year I was a co-trainer in a T-group; in my fourth year I joined the T-group staff.

In the mid-fifties we added some organization learning to the program through a total system simulation called "Regional City," a two-day event. Also in the mid-fifties, NTL expanded its activities to present programs for managers in business. The program was held at Arden House, the Averill Harriman estate on the Hudson River north of New York City. Here we started with a community simulation called the Arden Company. The rest of the program was T-group-based, with special interest groups in the afternoons.

Attendees had a powerful experience. Their suggestions that their bosses needed the same training drove a senior executives program. That in turn inspired presidents labs, conducted at glamorous resorts for CEOs and very senior executives; these have continued until the present.

Laboratory Education Goes to Europe

In 1953, Gordon Lippitt, then deputy director of NTL and previously the program director of the White House Conference on Children and Youth, took a leave from NTL to join the staff of the European Productivity Center in Paris. President Harry Truman had created the Truman Doctrine and the Marshall Plan to implement it. The mechanism for carrying out the plan was an agency within the state department called the Foreign Operations Administration. Under this plan, if a country determined a need for agricultural equipment for farms, for example, it could, through a country-managed productivity agency set up by the FOA, apply for the funds to buy the tractors or other equipment. The United States would advance 90 percent of the cost of the purchases, that, it was hoped, could be made from U.S. manufacturers, resulting in a win-win deal.

All the activities had been in machinery and technology. Lippitt convinced the people in charge to conduct an experiment transferring the technology of leadership training to a country in Europe, through conducting some workshops and developing some indigenous capacity to do further training in leadership using the laboratory method. A four-person team of NTL folks was selected. Lee Bradford, the NTL director, and I were from the staff. We were supplemented by two people who had been through the programs, were supporters, and were competent to train a group: Elbert Burr, vice president of personnel at Monsanto Chemicals Co. in St. Louis, and Robert Hood, my friend and client from Ansul Chemical. I was designated team leader, mainly because I did not have another full-time job and could devote time to the planning and logistics.

Austria, which at that time was under Allied control and had a coalition government, was selected as the test site for the program. Areas of the country had been allocated to each of the four powers: the United States, Russia, France, and the United Kingdom. Vienna was an open city; its administration rotated each month between the four occupying powers.

A design was created with the support of the head of the FOA mission in Austria, Biff Gale, who was sympathetic to the plan. There would be three two-week programs, conducted by the four of us, with four Austrian counterparts, whom we would be training to take on follow-up activities. The first program would be for top government, top industry, and top labor people. We would conduct it with our Austrian colleagues mostly observing. The second program was for middle managers in each of the three sectors. In this one, the Austrians and Americans shared the leadership. The third program, which was for first-line supervisors and union shop stewards, would be conducted by the Austrian staff, with the Americans as observers and coaches.

This experience was really a "trip," in many senses of the word. After we were officially appointed, we were sent to Washington for an administrative clearance and briefing. We also had to undergo a security clearance. The state department people in Washington made it clear that this whole project was not to their liking, but they had to let us do it. We were booked to fly to Paris, where we would get a thorough briefing from the FOA regional office before we went to Vienna, where our design planning sessions would be held.

As the only member of the team who had been to Europe (for two weeks the previous year to attend the coronation in England), I was considered the expert on travel. I made sure that all the team members knew about personal security, particularly about protecting their passports. We flew to Paris first-class on a plane with sleeper bunks and began to feel like VIPs. Upon our arrival in Paris for our one-day briefing, we were quickly disabused of our VIP status. And I quickly undermined my role as travel expert. After our overnight flight from New York (sixteen hours in those days), we checked into the hotel that had been booked, and we had the remainder of the day to rest and see Paris. The briefings were to start the next morning at 9 A.M. After a full day of briefings, we would then entrain to Vienna at ten that night.

On that first day, we napped and went out to dinner, winding up in a nightclub in the Saint-Germain district. The wine had flowed steadily, so we were having a good time and finally returned to our hotel about 2 A.M. When I woke up, feeling like I had two heads, the first thing I did was to check for my passport. It was missing! I frantically went through all my clothes and papers. I tried to reconstruct the previous evening. I had someone from the hotel check. No passport.

I was embarrassed, guilty, and scared. I had to tell my colleagues and the people at the state department what had happened. We were already barely welcome, and this would really hurt everybody. But there was no choice. I went to the briefing and explained the situation. After initial reactions of horror and frustration, the officials told me I probably could not leave with the team that night, but they would try to get me a temporary passport in time to go with them.

While my colleagues were being briefed, I spent twelve hours at the surete (police) at the U.S. Consulate, where they undertook to obtain a priority temporary passport. I spent the day waiting in one office or another, and I had nothing to eat. I could barely speak the language. At eight o'clock that night they gave me the temporary passport. I grabbed a sandwich, went to the hotel, picked up my things, and joined the group to go to the train station.

We had fine quarters on the Ahlberg Express, the evening version of the Orient Express, but I was so exhausted that I fell asleep instantly. The train passed through Luxembourg and Switzerland before it reached Austria. About seven in the morning immigration officials came aboard, checked my passport, and left. Then I opened my suitcase to take out some underwear—and found my original passport. I had hidden it in a pair of shorts!

So now I had two passports and a new host of problems. Who should I tell? Which passport was valid? The officials had canceled the original when they gave me the temporary. When we got to Vienna I had to disclose the whole story to Biff Gale, who was anything but pleased. He had to start proceedings for a new permanent passport. This was the beginning of our "helping hand" trip to Austria.

Even beyond my inauspicious arrival in the country, we soon found that we were seen as a nuisance group: the officials had to worry about our security; we had to be taken care of; the Austrian productivity people had reluctantly accepted the idea of having a leadership workshop. (All the participants were leaders already.) The embassy in Vienna was furious at our being there. During the sensitive four-power occupation period, they did not need a bunch of crazy human relations trainers doing a program that required facilities, staff, and support. We had a cool and almost unfriendly briefing from the embassy staff in Vienna and were given a space in the consulate for our planning.

Our first night in Vienna, after we were finally established in our rooms at about midnight, El Burr and I decided to stroll about the town for a bit (there was lots of nightlife to be found). On a side street we saw the neon sign for the Club Monseigneur. We went in. There was a tiny room with a small bar up front, a main room with people sitting on a banquette, and the most glorious music you could imagine being performed by a six-piece gypsy orchestra. It was the club of Koszce Antal—the king of the gypsies. We sat down and were offered the only thing they served—champagne and almonds. I was hypnotized by the music. Briefings were scheduled the next morning at nine. Burr decided to go back to the hotel at about two; I stayed on until four o'clock.

For the next week, while we were preparing the programs to be held at Linz, I would attend the briefings and plant visits all day, sleep for a couple of hours in the evening, and return to the club and stay up half the night. I had not been too popular with the local U.S. bureaucrats before, but now I was an embarrassment to them. My colleagues were embarrassed but professionally quiet.

After a week we went to Linz, an hour's train ride east of Vienna. In what was a learning experience for all of us, we spent several sessions preparing to work as a training team. We had to learn new skills and ways of functioning. For example, the interpreters had been trained and were competent in translating—taking the words from one language and saying them in another. But what we needed was real interpreting, that is, saying the *meaning* of one language in another language. The working language and most of the talk would be German; our interventions, in English, would be used much less of the time. We learned that summaries and other matters written on the blackboards or flipcharts had to be in German. How the languages transmitted the meaning was important. For example, "democratic leadership" could not simply be translated into *demokratische fuehrerschaft*. We needed the meaning interpreted and, in some cases, we had to invent words and phrases.

We had designed four teams. The original idea was to have two trainers and two interpreters. As we began working together, the interpreters became part of the training staff.

The daily design for the workshop was as follows. In the morning, we would start with a plenary session, which would include announcements, a bridge from the day before, and a theory session such as communications and decision-making processes. From ten until noon we would meet in the basic learning groups, which were unstructured. After a break for lunch, we would start with a lecture session, then another learning group session. In the last part of the afternoon, the trainers would leave, and four new groups—each composed of members from the four learning groups—would meet to discuss the day in German and give any feedback to the staff.

We started the program following that design. The learning group began their work. For the American team it was as much learning as teaching. For example, people tended to address each other by title and name—Herr Doctor Engineer Smith—hardly the level of openness one wanted in a T-group or lab learning group. It would take days for norms to change to more informal methods of salutation in a process led by the Austrian trainers and interpreters.

One of our biggest communication problems surfaced on the second or third day. We had developed what we considered a brilliant design invention by creating feedback or community groups. The agenda was for the participants, with no staff present, to critique the day and send any feedback either on the program or the management to the staff. Representatives from each of the groups would meet with the Austrian training staff to summarize and pass on their feedback. After dinner the entire staff would meet; the Austrians would pass their feedback along to us.

The first activity of the following morning would be our response to the feedback from the night before. For the first three days we got nothing—not one bit of feedback. We were aware of the cool behavior of the participants toward us, but we were unprepared for no dialogue or comments. We pushed our Austrian colleagues, but they said they could get nothing from the representatives except comments on trivial things such as facilities or coffee breaks. We were very frustrated.

On the fourth day the Austrian staff gave us a message from the participants. It was something like this: "Who do you think we are? Dumbbells? We have had American 'experts' do workshops before. We know how they work. They tell us, 'This is the way we do it in the U.S., and we hope it will be useful to you.' You people are asking us, 'What are our problems and issues?' We know you are CIA spies!"

We were flabbergasted. How could we respond to that feedback? We already had low credibility. The staff stayed up late that night developing a response and selecting a spokesperson. We decided on

Bob Hood. Among the four of us, he had the most credibility. He was perceived as a practical line manager, with no axe to grind; his style was laid back, mid-western, low key. If any of the American staff could be heard, it was Bob Hood.

The next morning he gave our response. "We've heard what you said. We understand, based on your previous experiences, how you might well feel the way you do. There is nothing we can say to convince you that we are not with the CIA, or that we are all civilians with no governmental connections who have been asked to come here to help you in your own leadership training by sharing our experience and learnings."At the opening session we had been introduced only as the faculty for the program; our backgrounds had seemed irrelevant. In Hood's reintroduction at this point, he described our backgrounds and present positions in the United States (corporate president, personnel vice president, applied behavioral scientists). He set forth in some detail who we were and where we came from in hopes of allaying their fears that we were CIA. The group listened politely. There was no discussion; there were no questions. We felt we had tried to connect but had not made much progress. We were heavy hearted as we left the general session and went to our learning group rooms for the morning session.

A remarkable coincidence that evening led to a breakthrough in our relationship. A tasting party for the new wines of that year was being held at a restaurant in Linz. The participants had all been invited, as had the Austrian staff and interpreters. Our Austrian colleagues somehow persuaded the sponsors of the event to invite us, which they did, somewhat reluctantly.

After some wine had been "tasted," someone started singing. Pretty soon a sing-along developed. One of the interpreters, a Hungarian woman, jumped on a table and started to dance to a gypsy tune. The singing grew more animated. Someone started yodeling. Several others joined in. Thanks to my singing experience both in college and in a glee club, I felt comfortable joining the singing and the yodeling. At first I got some startled looks, then polite acceptance, and before long full membership in the singing. Other staff joined in and we had a great evening.

The next morning the feedback was heard. An open discussion followed, and we began to be a community. By the time this first two-week workshop ended, the project team had become personae grata with the FOA and U.S. Embassy people, and with the Austrian Productivity Center in Vienna. It seemed we had avoided what might have been a disaster and a blot on international relations.

A second workshop was then given for middle managers in industry, labor, and government. In this program the American team and Austrian trainers were co-leaders. We held clinics after each group meeting and staff clinics in the evenings to help the Austrians prepare to conduct the third workshop. This third program was for first-line supervisors (*meister*) and shop stewards (*betriebsraete*). The Austrian staff conducted the whole program. The Americans sat in the back of the meeting rooms and held clinics with them to help them evaluate the sessions and plan subsequent ones.

Overall the project was deemed a success. It had enough impact that the following year the FOA arranged for the European Productivity Agency to send teams of applied behavioral scientists and trainers—four people from each of nine countries—to the United States for six months to observe leadership training programs at NTL and at UCLA to get ideas for their own work.

My NTL Family

It was during my early years at NTL and this European experience that some of my strongest NTL bonds were forged. Three of these were with Lee Bradford, Kenneth Beene, and Edith Whitfield Seashore.

Leland Bradford: My Guide Through NTL

Lee Bradford was one of three founders of NTL and was its director for the first twenty years. Before his NTL appointment he had been director of the adult education division of the National Education Association. When I first attended the NTL program, I was fortunate to be in a group that Lee led. One outcome for me was a tremendous respect for the man. I was very honored when he offered me the opportunity to return the next year on the staff to be in charge of the large meetings program and assist as a trainer with a skill practice group.

Lee and his wonderful wife, Marty, had open houses after the evening meetings. Most faculty would go over there for a drink and what became interesting discussions. People would share experiences from the significant events of the day, discuss how lab learning was being accepted, and discuss the learning community and adult education. I literally sat at the feet of these great minds as they discussed, debated, developed new theories, and heatedly discussed the world situation and politics (these were the Joe McCarthy days). I felt very humble and inadequate alongside these thought leaders and gurus—and lucky to be there.

Lee never let me be forgotten. He would engage me, ask my opinions, treat me as if I mattered. Through his behavior, other staff began to respect my contributions. Even though I had none of the formal training or experience the others had, I was accepted as a full-fledged member of the staff. Lee continued to encourage me to challenge myself. He took the enormous gamble of letting me lead a T-group—the core part of the program. T-group leaders needed to have clinical credentials. The responsibility was awesome, since no one could predict what might happen to people in an unstructured setting.

Lee always respected my practical side. He encouraged me to do some consulting with the central staff. In the mid-fifties, I was appointed to the NTL board. I served on that and future boards for almost twenty years, the last several as chair of the executive committee of the board.

As NTL matured, the single core program—the T-group—was augmented and modified, and new programs were added on large system and community dynamics. In the mid-sixties, there was a philosophical and physical split among staff. Those who believed in the personal growth aspect of the learning as primary, mostly California clinicians, broke away to create their own programs in sensitivity training. Some of the original staff were interested in systems thinking, complex change, and the social-psychological aspects of groups. Others were interested in therapy, healing, and personal growth.

While these camps fought each other, Lee managed to glue the system together and tolerate a wide variety of different programs. His ability to support different approaches, including those he didn't like, kept the institution together. Throughout this time Lee treated me with respect and caring. He could accept my ideas and began depending on me for some institutional management. I moved up to a senior position in the institution.

Over the years we became good friends. Lee and Marty and my wife, Lee, and I saw a lot of each other, almost like family. They had "adopted" me in the fifties. I was like an uncle to their son, David, who helped me with the audiovisual work when he was a child. Later, he sat in as an observer in my groups and went on to college and Stanford University, where he is now a professor and a consultant.

In the fifties, my wife and I would invite the entire NTL population of about fifty people over to our camp on weekends, half on Friday and half on Saturday, for a barbecue dinner. My wife, who was working in New York, would buy a batch of filets from her butcher. I would buy the beer. People would bring the stuff down the trail from where they parked their cars to our cottage on the lake. We would figure the costs, and someone would function as financial officer to collect everyone's share. We would have drinks plus lake activities—swimming, canoeing—and then Lee would cook the steaks and we'd sit around the big fire eating. Soon someone would start the singing, which would go on into the evening. The staff had a permanent invitation to these parties, so Lee and

Marty usually came. They fell in love with the lake and wanted to buy some property; unfortunately, there wasn't much available.

In 1965 my cottage burned to the ground in a lightning storm. I was able to buy some more land where the house had been. I then sold the half-acre I also owned on the point next to that land to Bradford and his extended family friend, Kenneth Benne. We all became neighbors, as well as friends and colleagues.

Lee Bradford spent his summers at the lake until his death. His wife continued to spend summers there until illness made it impossible. Their son, who had grown up there, bought the property and now summers there with his family.

Lee Bradford was my first true mentor. I miss him still.

Kenneth Benne: Mentor, Guide, Friend, and Neighbor

I met Ken Benne in 1950, long before he and his partner, Paul Blackwood, had their house built on the point next to my property in Maine, at the same time and by the same contractor as the Bradfords. I soon learned that he was one of the three founders of NTL. I also learned to respect and love him, as did everyone else who came in contact with him. Ken died a few years ago. Although burdened with serious heart disease, he had continued to participate at NTL, and in other work, with high energy. He was probably the most loved person in the history of NTL.

Ken was a social philosopher and the resident wise man on the Bethel staff. He had strong convictions and very strong opinions but could always be influenced by other opinions. His knowledge was vast: he could win the Jeopardy game, hands down. Such vast knowledge and conceptual skill would have frightened me in some people, but not in Ken. He was warm, caring, reliable, and always available for advice or guidance. He always treated me with respect and made me feel both worthy and competent. He encouraged me in my training work and in my writing. We collaborated on the early change agent programs at Bethel. He was a great partner on a faculty or training team. We were on the same staffs at Bethel, at

Arden House for the first management work conferences, and at various workshops in a number of settings over the years.

Ken founded and directed the human relations program at Boston University. His ex-students are all leaders in the field today. Miriam Ritvo, whom I have known since her graduate student days, is among those who made significant contributions both to the training field and to society.

A couple of years before his death, Ken produced a bibliography of his publications. It was the size of a small book—seventy pages or so. When he moved his base to Maine, he built a building adjoining his cottage and installed his library, which was then over six thousand books. His library has now been willed to the University of Kansas, where it will enrich their collection.

Ken spent his summers at the lake until he died. In the winter he and Paul had a flat in Washington, near a number of other NTL faculty friends. He was a great neighbor as well as a mentor and a wonderful friend. He was a regular attendee at our weekend parties at the cabin in Maine. He was also a committed songfest participant. He knew every song that could possibly be sung. As a trainer and guide, Ken was a master at turning people's competitive energy into a collaborative mode. But when it came to singing, it was another story. He was a fierce competitor over which song to sing and a collaborator on the singing itself. Just as Lee Bradford had to have his golf game at 3:30 every afternoon, Ken had to have his songfest every evening. I was happy to oblige.

Edith Whitfield Seashore: Friend and Colleague

Edie Whitfield has been a significant friend and "family" since 1950. We first became friends at Bethel in 1950, at the NTL program. Years later, when I started Conference Counselors with no money and no clients, Edie volunteered to help me get started and to work with me as a colleague. She went on with her own consulting work, and she worked as an NTL staff member during the early fifties. We kept in close touch. Later, when I replaced the name Conference

Counselors with Richard Beckhard Associates, my practice was large enough to support some associates. I asked Edie to join me. She and two others, Aaron Feinsot (now dean in NYU Extension), and Hugh Gyllenhaal (now deceased) began to work with me. The business did not grow as fast as the overhead, and I had to end my arrangement with the two men. Edie stayed on and took on several of my clients.

Edie began to develop her own practice. She married Charles Seashore, then a young professor and consultant. They have worked together and separately—both with highly successful consulting practices—to this day. Edie and Charlie also became central figures in NTL. They bought a big house in Bethel, which serves as an extension of the NTL campus. Programs are held there from May to October. When Lee Bradford retired, Charlie became part of a trio of directors and Edie was on the staff. A few years later, she became president of NTL and guided it through its second most turbulent and growthful period. Today, Edie and Charlie are the spirit of NTL to the townsfolk of Bethel.

We have remained like sister and brother for over forty years. Although we don't see much of each other, during the summers we visit them at Bethel, and they come out to the lake. It always seems as if nothing has happened between visits.

Learnings Along the Way

I learned a lot in those years, much that was relevant specifically to laboratory learning and training and much that would be relevant to subsequent aspects of my career. I learned that I would never be able to work outside my home country without consciously trying to understand the host culture in which I was working. And I learned the importance of paying close attention to relationships, both personal and professional.

3

Relationships
Balancing the Personal-Professional System

Until I started as a staff member at NTL, I had never given much thought to the subject of relationships and their interdependence with work. Certainly I had never considered the interdependence of professional and personal relationships.

In my childhood years I had only one close personal relationship. There was no logical reason for Wesley Randles and me to be buddies. Wesley was everything I wasn't. He was tall, well over six feet; I was barely over five feet. He was mechanically inclined; anything I touched broke. He was not interested in intellectual subjects; I was. When we were Boy Scouts and getting merit badges, his were for woodworking and pathfinding; mine were for civics and citizenship. But we were real pals. My parents invited him to join us for summers at camp. His ham radio setup was on our front porch. Our house was his main home (he was an orphan).

Most of the students at Pomona in the thirties came from well-to-do families. Their tuition was paid by their parents. They lived in first-class dorms that were not inexpensive. A small number of students could not afford the tuition and housing fees but wanted to attend this type of school. To deal with this, Pomona had a generous scholarship program, work grants, and alternative housing in a much humbler building called Smiley Hall. (Cynical students called it Smelly Arms.) I got along with my roommates there, although we had little in common. They were athletes, participating in all sports. I was in the dramatics and music activities.

I was not much of a joiner and had few close relationships. I was not pledged for any of the local fraternities. My friends, none close, were colleagues in drama and music and other activities. My need to earn everything except my tuition money by working in everything from the dining room to the theater left me little time for developing close relationships. In addition I was shy, partly because of my short stature and non-macho self-image.

My next significant relationship started several years after college. One of my Pomona classmates, Jack Wylie, had entered Harvard Medical School. I was in New York, stage managing and acting in "The Male Animal" on Broadway. Gene Tierney was in the cast, a role that led her into movie stardom. Jack was crazy about theater. He heard that I was connected with a Broadway hit and arranged to come to see it. Afterward I took him backstage and had him meet some of the cast. He "fell in love" with Gene Tierney. (She did not reciprocate. In fact, she knew him only as my college chum.) Jack arranged to come down from time to time, to see the show or another show and join me for a night out.

Jack went on to become a surgeon, later a vascular surgeon, and became world famous when he developed a procedure for repairing the carotid artery. After his residency, he joined the surgical staff at the University of California Medical Center in San Francisco. He had married one of his nurse assistants, Sarah; they had three children.

In 1955, a consulting assignment took me to California, and I went to visit them. That was the beginning of a relationship that lasted all Jack's life and continues with Sarah today. Like Wesley Randle, Jack and I had a deep affection for each other even though we were complete opposites. He was very tall; I was very short. He was a scientist; I was a theater director. He had amassed wealth; I got paid only when I worked, and I had very little savings. Jack's hobby was sailing; I only knew motorboats. On several of my visits, he took me on day sails in San Francisco Bay.

That made it easy to agree to go along with him one December in 1977 when he was going to charter a sailboat in the Caribbean for a week's cruise. About a month before we were to start the trip, Jack was called to the Far East to attend to some dignitary and had to cancel the trip. My wife, Elaine Kepner (whom I had married in 1975, a year after Lee's death) and I decided to go anyway. We would have a captain and a cook, and we could learn more about sailing. That was the start of a tradition, a December charter with the Moorings Co. in Tortolla, British Virgin Islands; 1997 is my twentieth year. The tradition was interrupted only when I had heart surgery in 1988.

So eventually Jack and I had a love of sailing in common. But there remained another significant difference: he was left-brain-driven; my right brain is dominant. When I went into the consulting and training field, Jack found what I did even more strange than my theater work. What did people's emotional life and work have to do with reality? What indeed.

Personal to Professional

When I became associated with NTL at Bethel, I discovered a whole new quality of relationships. The leadership, the staff, the intimate and powerful relationships they developed from the shared experience of the T-group and other activities—all combined to show me the intertwining of professional and personal relationships.

This concept was reinforced later as I consulted with Robert Hood, CEO of Ansul Chemical. As discussed in the next chapter, I stayed at his house, came to know his family, and became aware of the many dimensions of the man. We became real friends. We were in close touch for thirty years, and we still correspond.

Long-term friendships emerged from my next two consulting clients as well. Working with Roger Sonnabend during the sixties, as he created a vital and brilliantly managed hotel chain, the Hotel Corporation of America (HCA), was very stimulating. Again, the personal relationship that blossomed was a powerful experience. I began to know and work with the Sonnabend family; I became a friend and a counselor to Roger and to his brothers and their spouses. My clients were both HCA, the company, and the Sonnabend family.

I found myself in a similar situation when working with George Raymond, chairman of the Raymond Company, a materials-handling company that manufactured forklift trucks. His was a small company of about seven hundred employees when I first knew it. Even as a one-plant operation, it was the principal employer in Greene, a village in the northwest corner of New York State. Raymond's father had founded the company and had built it into a several-million-dollar enterprise. Raymond had grown up in the business, rising to vice president of sales, and had recently become president. His father had retained the board chairmanship; he was still very active in the business and in guiding his son.

I first met Raymond at meetings of the Young Presidents' Organization (YPO) through Bob Hood, then when his wife Cindy participated in a T-group workshop that I had set up, and then again when he participated in a leadership program that Bob Blake and I staffed. In that program, we were trying out the ways participants could use the Blake-Mouton Managerial Grid Program (described in detail in Chapter Four). This new grid organization development program had been created as a training program to increase managers' skills and understanding of their own leadership style, for team building, and for intergroup relationships.

Raymond was strongly affected by the experience. He was committed to developing a team management rather than carrying on the centralized, autocratic leadership style of his father. He asked me to facilitate a retreat meeting of the team, at which they would be discussing top team functioning and management strategy. I suggested that the group needed to look at both personal relationships and their interaction with the team workings. Raymond agreed.

As a mechanism for developing open and honest communications, he decided to use the Blake grid methodology, where the team members could share perceptions about each other's style values and challenges. He contracted with Blake to analyze the findings from the preliminary work. I then used this analysis to get the discussion going in what was a high-impact event. The management team (composed of Raymond and the vice presidents of marketing, manufacturing, finance, and research and development) agreed to meet at least once a month to continue this type of activity and asked me to attend the follow-up session. This led to an arrangement whereby I met with the team every third month to look at how the team was functioning and what needed changing or improvement, to review strategy, and to plan interventions that would help them become more effective. This worked for all of us. My relationship with the company lasted over twenty-five years and through many changes.

In my visits to Greene, I stayed at George Raymond's house. I became close with his family and a part of their extended family. I watched the children grow up and the family flourish. When he lost his wife, Cindy, I helped the family through the critical period. The management team asked me to help bridge the family grief and the dynamics of the group. Our personal relationship deepened. Raymond treated me as an older brother and relied on me to help him through the next steps in his life. We have kept in close touch and have a deep bond that has continued long after the client relationship ended.

All this time, I was developing lasting relationships and becoming a family business consultant, although I didn't yet think of it that way. Slowly, my experiencing led to conceptualizing. I realized that in each client's organization, I was working with a system: a

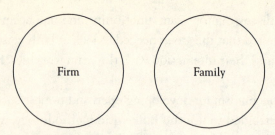

Figure 3.1. Family Firm System.

family firm system with two subsystems—family and firm (see Figure 3.1).

As with its controlling shares ownership, the family could decide the fate of the business. The company's CEOs were heads of both business and family; thus they were subsystems. So an accurate depiction of the total system would have three subsystems: the CEOs, the family, and the firm (see Figure 3.2).

The System of Relationships

In thinking of these relationships, rather than only experiencing them, I realized that I too was involved in a variety of relationships,

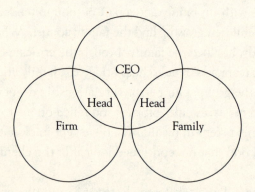

Primary Objectives

Profitability and Growth   Maintenance and Fulfillment

Figure 3.2. The CEO in the Family Firm System.

sometimes with the same people. I was trying to manage each of the relationships in ways that would nurture them, while keeping my life in balance. In thinking about this I used a family as a metaphor. The father has individual relationships with his spouse, each of his children, and the children as a group. He has to be aware of the tensions between autonomy and interdependence with each subset. He has to adjust his behavior toward each person and group in ways that are appropriate to that relationship.

This concept drove my thinking further into the issue of managing relationships. For me, I discovered that all life is a series of relationships that must be managed. This doesn't mean that I should control them but that I should create conditions for their survival and growth. This became a paradigm that guided my thinking, my degree of commitment to each relationship I had. I understood that I myself was a system, with all sorts of external and internal demands on me. Each domain or relationship was saying, at least implicitly, "We want you to . . . behave in certain ways, hold certain values and beliefs, relate in certain ways." Not the least of these demands came from my own values and prejudices, of which I had been blissfully unaware.

Using the *open system planning model,* I created a picture of my personal and professional system (see Figure 3.3). The circle in the center—representing me—had several selves: consultant, teacher, writer-editor, faculty member at MIT and NTL, and learner. Interacting with those were demands from my wife, my Shangri-la in the Maine woods, my ethics, my values, and my lifestyle. My life's challenge was to manage all of these interfaces in a way that I could ensure good physical and mental health. Systems thinking helped me to understand and balance the various relationships and demands.

I began thinking about everything in this way. Client Robert Hood was in the middle of a complex system of demands and roles. He was the owner of his company, the CEO of the company, the head of his family, a key figure in his community, a member of an

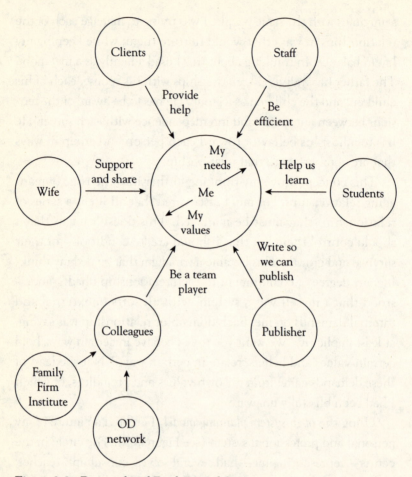

Figure 3.3. Personal and Professional System.

industry (the fire prevention field). He had competing demands for his time and energy. His own personal core values were another force on him. He had to anticipate the consequences of his acts on all parts of the system—the effects on the family, on the management, on the community. From my systems perspective, I was able to help him manage these various forces. He later said that was one of the most helpful aspects of my consulting.

I began seeing all clients as part of social systems. I realized that the organization system is not just the formal organization. The

organization system includes the various constituencies that interact with its work: the board of directors, the employees, and sometimes their unions, the community, and the media—to name some
key ones. Systems thinking became for me a whole new way of looking at reality. It has been another part of my core process for thirty-
five years and was directly linked to establishing myself as a
organizational consultant and my connection to organizational
development, described in the following chapters.

In implementing this concept professionally, at the beginning
of every consulting assignment I contracted with clients on the
ground rules for our relationships and the conditions for terminat-
ing it. These contracts were oral agreements and served to establish our relationship rather than "the deal" we had struck. To
communicate that organization change takes time, I made it clear
that the time frame could not be any less than five years; however,
either party could terminate the arrangement with two month's
notice. These ground rules worked: they gave us time to build
mutual trust and confidence, to establish and build feedback mechanisms, and to work together as partners. They also allowed us to
budget my services on an annual basis and not have to renegotiate
for each project. In short, I learned to establish contracts or agreements with colleagues, whether I was working with them, training,
or consulting.

Systems Thinking as a Tool

What I was doing in all these relationships had derived from what I
had learned at NTL about systems thinking. From listening to some
of my senior colleagues talk about their theories, I learned to look
at individuals, groups, and organizations as systems. According to a
theory of open systems being developed in the early sixties by James
Clark, Charles Krone, and Will McWhinney at UCLA, it was postulated that for any change to be optimized, managers should think
in systems and strategic terms. There was great interest among

senior managements; many consulting firms began specializing in this as a service. I saw an opportunity for applying open systems theory as a diagnostic tool that could be used to prepare for making a strategic plan and developed a six-step model:

1. Identify the present demand system. Which domains were making demands on the management: competitors, unions, media, employees, family, self?

2. List current response pattern.

3. Look ahead two years, to a future without change by you. If you didn't do things very differently, what would the demand system look like then?

4. Project your ideal or desired condition for the same time frame.

5. Determine what behaviors would have to occur for you to reach the desired future condition.

6. Perform a cost-benefit analysis of these activities and feed this into your strategic planning process.

Managers found this a useful and orderly way of preparing for strategic planning. It was widely adopted and is still used today by many leaders as an aid in diagnosing the present state of an organization or team. This was just one of a series of tools that I was able to work on and use to help others over the years.

Significant Relationships

I have been blessed on my journey with a number of supporters, guiders, mentors, and role models. Their names and stories are integral to my life and are laced through the book. Six people in particular made a significant impact on my professional life; three I have discussed already: Leland P. Bradford, Kenneth Benne, and Edith Whitfield Seashore. To them and to Douglas McGregor, Marjan Schroeder, and Ivan Lansberg I will be forever grateful. I am honored to have had each of them as friends.

Douglas McGregor: My Champion, Role Model, and Friend

I first met Doug at NTL in 1950, when he came to "visit" the NTL program. At the time he was president of Antioch College and a friend of Lee Bradford. We struck up an acquaintance.

The next year Doug joined the staff of the first NTL management work conference, which was a program for managers in business. Because of my consulting experience I was asked to join the same staff. We became close colleagues and seemed a natural pair because we were the nontraditional members among the staff. Doug had a foot in both the academic and practical camps and was respected in both. He was my role model.

We soon discovered that we had in common a love for honky-tonk piano and singing. After the evening sessions, Doug and I would head for the lounge and grab a drink. Doug would play the piano and I would sing. It became a tradition: Doug and Dick, the tall and the short of it, providing the "entertainment leadership" after hours. We usually drew a crowd, but the major fun was just doing it.

Doug and his wife, Caroline (who attended workshops with him), and I became real friends. They came up to visit us in Maine. In the summers Doug and I were both faculty of the senior executive program, which NTL had started after the success of the management work conferences. Caroline and my wife co-conducted some women's programs at Bethel.

When we rebuilt our cottage in 1966, Caroline planted a larch in the front yard in memory both of Doug, who had recently died, and of the fallen cottage. We were very close to her until she died of cancer a few years later. At Doug's memorial, someone said, "He was a gardener. He loved to plant seeds and help the flowers grow." I was one of the lucky ones who sprouted under his guidance and care. He brought me to MIT, got me appointed lecturer (and reappointed, against custom), and taught with me until his untimely death. He was probably the best friend I had in my adult life.

Marjan Schroeder: My European Connection

Marjan came into my life in 1956. One of her assistants at the Netherlands Institute for Preventive Medicine had attended an NTL program the year before. He had recommended the program to her, and she attended it.

We became friends during that summer. Marjan taught me the meaning of friendship as I had never known it. Marjan was a big woman, with a deep voice and a commanding presence. Conversations with her were both stimulating and exciting. I wanted to deepen our friendship and to make some commitment to each other to be friends for life. In typical American fashion I was plunging from an acquaintanceship to a friendship to a best friend relationship. Marjan became increasingly uncomfortable as I pressed her for some long-term, platonic commitment. She finally explained to me that in her country, and in most of Europe, a person was lucky to have more than three friends in a lifetime. People are cautious in entering relationships, but when they do make a commitment, it is very deep. Americans tend to move fast into a relationship, but if it gets very deep or intimate they run away fast.

This was one of the major lessons of my life. It not only affected all future relationships, it helped me become aware of my own difficulties with intimacy beyond a certain level. It helped me understand how values differ across cultures. It also helped me to understand what a real friendship means. Marjan and I did become friends, and we remained so for the rest of her life. She was a special friend, one I really miss.

Marjan took me to Holland, where I worked for three years with the Dutch Trainers Group. She was my entry to Denmark, where I worked for years. I brought her to Cleveland, where she worked with the Gestalt Institute of Cleveland. I arranged for her to consult with my client, The Hotel Corporation of America.

Ivan Lansberg: Philosopher, Friend, and Client

I first met Ivan Lansberg of the Grupo Lansberg in Venezuela at an NTL presidents program. We got along well, and he invited me to come to Venezuela to do a presentation on managing change for the business leaders of the country. From that, I developed three clients: his firm and two other leading Venezuelan companies, all family businesses.

Over the years we became close personal friends. On trips to Venezuela, I stayed in his home. He and his family regularly came to New York for a few weeks at Christmas. Often we were the only non-Venezuelans at their New Year's Eve party.

Ivan is the closest to a true Renaissance man that I have ever known. He is an avid scholar, philosopher, writer, and teacher, and was an outstanding business executive. He was always learning. He was a wonderful mentor of his children and many other young people. He was a great influence on his country's moral and ethical life and is deeply admired and loved.

For me, he was and is a true and loving friend. He and Josette made me a member of their extended family. I mentored the children, particularly Ivan, Jr., whom I counseled as a graduate student, worked with as an adjunct to his program at Yale, and wrote with about family businesses in organization dynamics. Ivan, Jr. is now a distinguished colleague and leader in the family business field; we too enjoy an ongoing friendship.

Relationships: Finding the Balance

Beyond wanting to acknowledge some of my finest friends and colleagues, why do I bring them into this book here and in other chapters? How do these friendships relate to my life as a change agent? Clearly, I knew these people and had deep connections with them. Also as part of my early experience at NTL, I began to recognize the importance of being process-aware. First I recognized this in my head. Then, it became an organic part of me. In every interaction, I found myself both engaging in and observing the process. This became an important part of my helping clients in their development. Over time, I began to better understand the impact of relationships on the process. Of the many elements in observing groups or pairs process, the relationships of the participants was the most fundamental.

Again this started as cognitive awareness. As I moved up on the learning curve, I began to be aware of the fact that the managing of my relationships was the most important aspect of my being. I realized that my relationships to loved ones, colleagues, students and mentors, clients and friends, all required conscious managing. That was a powerful insight. It has been a part of my core process for years.

4

Becoming an Organization Consultant

A s an NTL trainer, I was functioning in a facilitating capacity. I was there to help with managing the learning process and to help the participants develop an awareness of their individual and group processes. My primary role was to create the conditions under which people can learn. Outside of NTL, I was still functioning as a large meetings expert. But I had very few clients. People were not lined up waiting for me to help them improve their meetings. My activities were direct applications of my expertise. I had yet to complete the metamorphosis from expert to consultant.

And I had no real marketing strategy. I'm sure many readers who have started their own consulting practice have faced the same problem. The tension between being your own boss, with all the freedom that implies, and having to face the economic reality that if you don't work you don't get paid is quite stressful. I decided to offer some public workshops on conference planning and meetings improvement as a way of acquiring some clients while receiving some income. From these, I found a few clients who wanted help with their meetings. I conducted in-house workshops and consulted with some client managers on how they could improve their meetings. I did not differentiate my roles. I did everything an expert does: fix the problem, help the client increase capacity, and educate.

Transitioning to Consulting

My first explicit consulting contract was in 1951 with Bob Hood at the Ansul Chemical Company in Marienette, Wisconsin. My assignment was as an expert: I was to conduct several meetings improvement workshops for managers. In addition to my input on meetings, Hood wanted some help on communications policy and practices, on the functioning of his top team, and on his managerial style. I wasn't an expert on any of these subjects. What Hood wanted was to reflect, discuss, and share some of the matters that were of concern that he did not feel comfortable discussing in any depth with his staff and managers. I began to be aware that as an "outsider," I brought a different perspective. (I had to: I knew nothing about his business.) I could listen, try to reflect what I'd heard, suggest alternatives on actions, raise "dumb" questions.

In the evenings at his home, we would explore ways that I could help with other issues, which we discussed as they came up in no logical order. Hood wanted to improve the quality of communication between levels, particularly between supervisors and the workforce. He wanted to improve the functioning of the top team, particularly the degree of openness and trust among the members. He was concerned about the middle managers' commitment to development and change. He discussed whether the organization structure was the most appropriate. He was concerned about relations with the board (which he controlled), about relations with the community (Ansul was the biggest employer in town), and about maintaining a proper balance among his many roles.

As his trust in me developed, he shared his more personal concerns about his adequacy as a leader. He was the principal owner, the president, the head of his family. He was a parent and a spouse. We had many profitable discussions about the tensions of being both owner and top manager. Most helpful to him, I discovered, was being able to think with him about his priorities, frustrations, and concerns about the personal risks involved in various aspects of his job and roles. If he was open with his managers, would they lose respect for him? Since he was the owner as well as president, would senior managers be willing to disagree with him or challenge him without fear of reprisal? How could he avoid playing favorites among his senior managers, even though he had different feelings about them? How could he communicate values and beliefs through the organization? An example he used was getting supervisors to refrain from punishing workers who made errors and, instead, to see what could be learned from errors. From having watched the organization work, I was able to point out that his norms and values were already functioning throughout the organization—and functioning well. His personal behavior, how he lived his values, had been a role model for many in the company.

My professional and personal relationship with Hood was my training school in consulting. It was my graduate education—and I was paid for it for over ten years. Probably I should have paid Hood. I had a living laboratory in which to develop a theory of consulting, to apply my theories, and to get the most relevant feedback as individual and organizational capacity increased. It was a perfect expression of a theme in my life story—doing and then learning—and was the foundation for much of the work I did throughout my career.

The experience with Hood and Ansul was frequent enough—I visited there monthly—and continued long enough for the learning curve to act in my favor. The referrals gave me some additional clients with similar problems. Some of these were Hood's fellow members of the Wisconsin chapter of the Young Presidents Organization (YPO). Their issues were similar to his. They had concerns about their work, their relationships, and their priorities. I began to see what problems are common to leaders. I was able to use my learnings to develop some concepts and frameworks that could help clients think about their issues.

Systems as a Conceptual Framework

As discussed in Chapter Three, in working with Hood I began to see the interdependency of the various parts of his world. There was the business that was Ansul. There was Ansul in an industry. There was Ansul as a financial asset of the Hood family. There were a number of organizational systems: the whole organization, the management team, the supervisors, the workers. There was a system of Ansul in the community. The community had an effect on company policies and vice versa. There were spouses, parents and children, extended family—the family system. Just as Bob Hood had to manage all these systems and his role within them, so did I as a consultant have to define both my work and my relationships with each of them.

From my NTL experiences, I had learned that in any interaction between individuals or within a group, there is the content or subject being discussed, and there is the process—the dynamics of the relationships between the participants and the group. How decisions are made, the communications and participation patterns, the norms or ground rules, the leadership style—are all process issues. As I worked with Hood and his colleagues, I realized that attention to process is a fundamental element of an effective consulting relationship.

I began to discover that my "expertise" was not only in the subjects such as meetings improvement but in the capacity to work with, support, advise, challenge, provide theory, and to share other experience. In other words, it was my expertise on the management of the processes that was of value. At the time, I was able to analyze the different kinds of help for the clients. They wanted

- To use my expertise, for example, in designing a team-building meeting or a new communications procedure

- Some coaching and help in solving problems (such as communication between levels) or making interventions (such as those that would improve how the top team functioned)

- Some input on others' experiences or findings

- Counseling on personal and interpersonal issues

From experiencing these requests at Ansul and subsequent client systems, I began to develop a conceptual framework that became a part of my own practice and that I was able to pass on to other consultants and students in subsequent years.

Acting as an Agent of Change

I realized that in both my consulting and training I was primarily facilitating change. In my client work, most of the issues on which I was consulting were change issues, some of personal change and growth, most connected to needed or desired organization change. I began to categorize the types of changes on which I worked as changes in

- Management style

- Relationships to the outside environment

- Operating policies and mechanisms

- The organization's culture (the way people are treated, including how decisions are made, what values should be driving the work, and so on)

In each of these types of changes, I was functioning as an agent of change, supporting the change manager or client who owned the problem. I was able to add value by my interventions, most of which were educational. I would use others' experiences to help the client understand how to cope. I would share theory and concepts with the client. I would conduct some educational activity in the early stages of our relationship.

This pattern was set with my first three major clients: Hood, Sonnabend, and Raymond. In each case, my entry into the system was with the president, and my very first work was in helping him identify the changes he wanted to make. In each case, my second intervention was some form of educational activity. With Hood and

Ansul it was a series of meetings clinics and then training in communication skills for the management group. With Raymond it was a series of team-building workshops with the management group, using NTL-type methods; later it was managerial grid workshops, conducted throughout the company. With Sonnabend and the Hotel Corporation of America, it was a series of one-week training sessions for the general managers and for headquarters staff heads, using laboratory learning methods. I conducted these with Ed Schein, my former NTL colleague, who was then professor of management in the organization behavior group at the School of Management at MIT. That work expanded into working with individual hotel leadership teams, redesigning the work, working with startup teams in new hotels, and working with staff-line relationships. The connections among the various projects became clear: they were all part of Roger Sonnabend's explicit strategy to make HCA the preeminent hotel chain in profitability, service, and organization effectiveness. His was a master plan to create a new state.

In working with these clients and others, my "place in the universe" became clearer. I was a change agent. I performed this in both consulting and training settings. My mission, my raison d'être, was to help other people and organizations become more effective and continue to grow. I never owned their problems. Instead, I always tried to help the people who did own them work on them and learn from the process of doing so. Finally, I had uncovered my specialty: the process of change.

The Change Model

In my first year at NTL, I had read the Lippitt, Watson, and Wesley book, *The Planning of Change*, and it had profoundly affected me. The authors described change as a process with three states: the future or changed state, the present state, and a getting-from-here-to-there state. I often used these states as a framework for helping CEOs manage some of the changes they were trying to achieve,

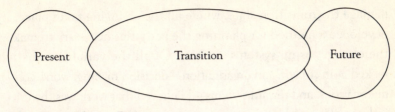

Figure 4.1. Change Process.

such as changing management style, changing the reward system, installing a communications system, and relocating decision making in the organization.

I began to think that this model of the process of change could be applied in all change situations. I built upon it to create a conceptual model—a *change management model*—for managing the change process. In the model, I described the three states of change as *future, present,* and *transition* (see Figure 4.1).

I used my own consulting and training experience as a basis for developing a way of managing each of the phases (see Figure 4.2). To manage and define the future state, I used the technique of scenario writing, that is, writing a description of the desired organization behavior in the changed state. To analyze the present state, I developed a series of diagnostic questions to assess the present state in the context of the desired state. The analysis includes an assessment of the attitudes and degree of commitment of key players, whose support would be necessary for the change to happen. To

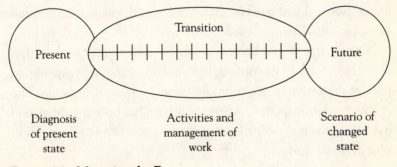

Figure 4.2. Managing the Process.

manage the transition state, where all the changing takes place, I developed a method for planning the activities necessary to make the change, using systems analysis. Of all the variables usually looked at in studying an organization—decision making, work, communications, and reward systems—I believed that work was the critical one. The work of the transition was not the same as that of the present state or the future state. I reasoned that if the work was unique, a structure must be dedicated to that work. I then posed the next steps in the model: defining the activities necessary during the transition state and developing a management structure to manage them.

I knew that having a good change plan was no guarantee that it would be implemented successfully. The commitment of a critical mass was needed for the change to occur. Getting commitment was a big step, one requiring a process. To that end, I developed a process for defining needed commitment of key players, without which the change could not happen. I developed a simple Commitment Chart (see Resource B) to assess necessary minimum commitment, current commitment, and the gap between them for the key players. The model also presents a series of strategies for getting the necessary minimum commitment. One of these strategies, called *responsibility charting* (see Resource B), was a method for resolving the "who does what to whom" kinds of questions that are often major issues in organizational change; with it, people could systematically decide who should behave how in a decision-making/authority dilemma. The technique is still widely used and has been, perhaps, the most used of my tools.

The change model became a part of all my future work, either as the basis for it or its context, both in consulting and teaching. In each of my various roles, it has been part of what defines me. The change model, adapted to different settings, has been my shtick and has helped me make contributions to my clients and to the fields in which I have worked.

Taking the Change Model to Large System Change

The change model was the conceptual framework for my work as my doing and learning continued. As will be discussed in Chapter Seven, for a large portion of my career, I taught change courses at MIT, often to students who were planning to go into consulting after their graduation. It seemed logical to me that the practicum model, using live cases, could also be applied in a professional development setting. I decided to transfer some of the content I was teaching about intervening in large complex systems and about consulting with organization management to a professional workshop on large systems change, NTL's summer program at Bethel. In the early 1970s, I conducted the first one-week workshop on consulting in large systems change; its focus was designing and facilitating change in large systems.

The workshop design was as follows. The core of the program would be self-selected learning/consulting groups. Each of the participants brought to the program a change effort in which they were personally involved. A good part of the program was receiving and giving help to fellow members on their own change efforts. This meant a lot of consulting practice, including exchange of their own "theories" of practice. In addition to the consulting groups, one or two afternoons were devoted to special interest groups. Participants could meet with colleagues who wanted to work on a specific issue. Subjects included entry issues, making an organization diagnosis, determining early interventions, and working with inside and outside partners. The third element of the program was input sessions in which the staff would present theories and concepts and participants could discuss applications to their work.

That first year, Ron Fry, my teaching assistant at MIT, was the staff. We managed to survive flak from the NTL management about a non-NTL member serving on the NTL faculty. The program was well received by the participants, most of whom had attended my earlier sessions. The second year, Edith Seashore joined me as staff. The third year I conducted the program with Carolyn Luckensmeyer and John Carter, both of whom were senior members of NTL. By then the program had its own momentum. Subsequently, other NTL trainers took over the program, which continues to be offered every summer at Bethel.

Years later I tried to codify my learnings in a working paper I wrote as part of a change course at MIT. In the paper, titled "The Dynamics of the Consulting Process in Large System Change," I look at the process (from the consultant's point of view) of helping with large system change.

Profile of My Consulting Experience

For most OD consultants their entry client into the system is in the human resources or personnel department. My experience was quite different. My first client was the president of his company, as was the case with the next four clients. This was due in large part to my connection with Hood, and his to the YPO. It was how I went on to learn about and interact with family businesses. My early work with Hood was especially key since, until 1965, most of my consulting practice was with family-owned businesses.

I recently did a brief summary of my client list from my beginnings as a consultant in 1952 to an arbitrary cutoff in 1972. The organizations with which I had a relationship over time are shown in Figure 4.3.

A common denominator of all of these contracts was having a relationship with the CEO. This allowed me to have input and influence at the center when needed. From my very first consulting assignment with Robert Hood at Ansul, I found myself consulting with both the leadership and with the organization as a whole. I learned on the job. Every client that hired me was concerned with changing something: the top team, the ways of work, external rela-

Company	Clients
Ansul Chemical Co., Marinette, Wisconsin	President and personnel
Hotel Corporation of America (HCA), Boston headquarters, Bermuda, London, and Milan	President and general managers
Raymond Co., Greene, New York	President and top team
Donut Corporation of America (DCA), New York	CEO
J. Lyons, Ltd., London	Owner/CEO, marketing director, and OD
Imperial Chemical Industries (ICI), London	CEOs, directors, and human resources managers
Procter & Gamble (P&G), Cincinnati headquarters	Manufacturing management, country boards, human resources, and president

Figure 4.3. A Sampling of Clients and Contacts.

tions, communication patterns. My task was to help clients with their issues. In doing that, I quickly learned to use my learnings about process to "guide" the interaction. From each experience I was gaining learnings that I could then use as interventions with the next client.

Principles of Practice

As my practice grew and my track record was generally positive, more opportunities appeared. I began to understand the nature of the consulting process, about which very little had been written at the time. One of my greatest assets, with each engagement, was to bring the learnings from other experiences to each new client. These soon distilled into a set of principles of practice.

Principle One: Learning

I became convinced that learning needed to be a part of any project; every intervention should be designed to be developmental. I would not take on a consulting contract unless I could learn from the experience. Also, I made it clear that training inside change agents, consultants, and trainers was a legitimate part of my consulting contract.

My work with Hood had taught me the value of treating the work with a client as a joint inquiry in which the stated goal is to combine the client's and consultant's resources to get the client's problems solved. An unstated but equally central goal is for both the client and consultant to learn. For the client it means increasing capacity in solving problems and personal growth. For the consultant it means learning how to provide real help, to control meeting one's own needs, to stay engaged, yet outside of the system.

As the years went on and I had more work than I could comfortably handle, my criteria changed. For me to take on a project, I had to see that it would improve the workplace conditions and opportunities for growth, see that I could learn from the experience, and know that I could add value.

Principle Two: Time Frame

A second principle was that the relationship could not be time-bound. This went against the norm: many OD consultants follow the practice of other consultants and take assignments on a project basis. They prefer projects that have beginnings and ends, in which results can be measured, at least generally. But I knew that change takes time. I wanted to have a few long-term relationships in which I could add value to the strategic thinking and planning of the leadership rather than simply oversee a number of short-term projects.

So the short-term projects that came my way, I referred to other OD consultants.

Principle Three: Feedback

A third principle was that continuing and periodic feedback must be part of the contract. Even if the client was comfortable with my work, I insisted on a scheduled "How are we doing?" session every few months and made it a condition of employment. Occasionally a client balked at paying for this. In one case I was unable to convince the client of the importance of these meetings—and I turned down the job.

Principle Four: Inside Connections

A fourth principle was that I needed to have a partnership relationship with a senior inside person in the HR staff who managed the logistics of my work. I needed to be explicit that my work was an extension of theirs and to maintain contact with them, even though I might be working on confidential and private material with some of the senior executives. The senior executives needed to know that I would maintain my professional relationship with that inside colleague.

Principle Five: Confidentiality

I would not discuss information obtained from one client in the system with other clients. There were two exceptions to this: (1) when I could assist in avoiding a serious problem by making leadership aware of the potential for trouble, and (2) in practice, I sometimes felt the need to have "professional discussions" with my inside partner. I made sure that other clients were aware of my position.

These principles have stood me very well in all aspects of my consulting career. For the past thirty years, a significant part of my professional work has been in professional development. In the past ten years, a major part of my practice has been coaching consultants. In these areas, the principles have stood the test.

Throughout my consulting work and my twenty-one years of teaching graduate students at the Sloan School at MIT, I have tried to pass the principles on. The large majority of students who took my courses are currently employed or are planning to become management consultants; I trust the principles have been useful to them as well.

Multiple Identities, Multiple Learnings

I have said that *consultant* is a generic title. Until an area of expertise is defined, there is no identity. In contrast, experts in marketing, financial planning, health and safety, and manufacturing are easy to identify. Expertise in business and organization management consulting is harder to pin down; OD consultants are harder yet to describe, even for one as closely linked to the field as I am.

The field's development, and my connection to it, are covered more thoroughly in the next chapter. It remains an evolving field. Until recently it was possible to differentiate auditing firms such as Arthur Anderson and Price Waterhouse from management firms such as McKinsey and Booz Hamilton. Organization development was differentiated from both these fields; the expertise was in human development and planned change. In recent years, the identities of all these specialties have become less clear. The big auditing firms and the management firms have added change practices to their lines of service.

The main identity of OD consultants—experts in change—is now a part of the identity of all management consultants. The reality is that today, organization leaders are demanding more from consultants than subject expertise. To provide the services demanded, organization consultants must become experts in consulting. The challenge will be to train other practitioners in consulting skills and to recognize that OD consulting is a process, not a profession.

5

Organization Development
Shaping the Field of Practice

In the early sixties my life was relatively stable. My consulting practice included two clients on retainers and produced enough income to pay the bills. My wife had a reasonably well-paying job as director of the camping division in the national office of the Girl Scouts. Rent from a small apartment in our house covered the mortgage payments. I was established as a senior practitioner—a fellow at NTL. I was part of the staff of other NTL programs including management work conferences, the program for senior executives, and later president's labs for corporation presidents. I was occasionally called upon to speak at chapter meetings of the Society of Management and the American Management Association. I had become somewhat visible as a specialist on change and change management, a subject that was of rising interest in the management community.

I had developed and tried out my model of change management with several clients, who had found it useful. And I was still finding my way, as was the field that would become organization development.

Antecedents of Organization Development

There is a long history of efforts to improve organization effectiveness, mostly through the increased productivity of workers. In the twenties, Frederick Taylor introduced "industrial engineering" as a method of improving efficiency. Mass production through the use of engineering methods made the United States the highest-producing country in the world. These efforts reached their peak during World War II, when an incredible effort produced an almost unbelievable materiel for a war machine. Systems were created that could produce maximum output from each worker. The attention was on doing the job; little attention was paid to the psychological or emotional needs of those who did the work. In contrast, the military did pay some attention to morale. The government even recruited behavioral scientists to attend to this aspect of work.

The concept of command and control and a hierarchy of authority was central to all management of tasks. For example, in designing the crew of a bomber, the most important role was the pilot's. So the pilot became leader of the crew. Originally that meant leading in all circumstances. But because of the multiple tasks involved—navigating, bombing, and so on—it became obvious that leadership would have to be in different roles at different times. The job of the captain became one of allocating leadership to the various crew members. The crew became a team. As the importance of team work became apparent and as the leadership role became more complicated—command at times, facilitation at others—the air force turned to psychologists for guidance on building team effectiveness.

After the war, when the economy boomed as the GIs returned with money to spend, the demands for production of goods increased quickly. To cope with this increased demand, industry tried to use the engineering approaches to productivity that had worked in the war. They were shocked to find that the workforce was no longer aligned with management in a common cause. People wanted more recognition and reward and shareout. There was a tremendous rise in union activity, as people realized that only through collective effort could they achieve a power balance with management.

The concept of leader or supervisor as boss and commander simply wasn't working. Leadership training for supervisors was necessary. Business executives first turned to the engineering methods of training that had worked before. They did not deal with the "human aspect." Programs of training were developed in which supervisors were told, "Be sure you say hello to the crew every morning. Keep track of birthdays. On Monday ask people how they spent their weekend." Manuals were produced; training departments were created and enlarged. Training became a major department in the personnel function.

Partly out of frustration with these training methods, the human relations training field was born: NTL and laboratory training were key aspects. Supervisory training was changed to leadership training and included self-awareness, skills in relating to others, and communication skills. There was a tremendous demand for leadership trainers in the early fifties. People with backgrounds in education and social work flocked to fill these positions; salaries were a lot higher than in the nonprofit sector. Opportunity was knocking.

Organization Development Is Named

As discussed in Chapter Three, over the years I had become close to Douglas McGregor. I worked with him in NTL management work conferences and later in senior executive programs. Doug had been the head of the industrial relations department of the School of Management at MIT during the forties. He left MIT to become president of Antioch College in Yellow Springs, Ohio. In the mid-fifties he returned to MIT, where he created an organization studies department in the school, which is now called the Sloan School of Management. In 1959, Doug was part of the core faculty of the Sloan Fellows Program. The program had been established in the early fifties, through a gift from Alfred Sloan, for high-potential mid-career managers, mainly engineers, to gain general management perspective and skills. In a one-year master's in management course at the School of Management, they could be exposed to the ideas and thinking of the impressive MIT faculty.

As a part of his research, Doug was working on a theory of management. He postulated that management behavior and styles were a function of the significant assumptions (beliefs) one had about the nature of human nature. For example, if managers believed that people were naturally lazy, their management behavior would be to manage against the laziness, by close supervision and control. If, on the other hand, they believed that people are naturally active—as behavioral science research had shown (Did you ever see a lazy baby?)—they would manage in a way that allowed people's natural energy to be released by changing the organization conditions, rules, or controls that were getting in the way.

Doug had presented his theory in a speech and article he delivered to a Sloan Fellows convocation. This article was expanded to become his 1960 book, *The Human Side of Enterprise*, a landmark work in management thinking. He called the traditional style Theory X and the science-supported assumptions Theory Y. Teaching supervisors to become coaches and controllers was one goal of a Theory Y approach. Letting workers set their own performance and development objectives was another.

Working on Culture Change

In 1959 Dewey Balch, the vice president of personnel at General Mills Company, initiated a culture change program throughout the company called *bottoms up management*. Some of the conditions the program was designed to achieve were: moving decision making down, installing communications mechanisms between organization levels, giving workers more say in the design and monitoring of their work, and moving the supervisory role from one of command and control to one of collaborative planning and support. Today, this would be called a reengineering effort.

Balch knew of Doug's work and invited him to consult with the implementation of the program. Doug knew of my strong interest in studying the change process and methods of managing change. He also was aware of my orientation toward systems thinking. He invited me to join him in the project; together we developed a series of interventions that included

- Top team goal setting and defining their role in the change

- Leadership training for all levels of management

- Performance improvement meetings with supervisors and workers

- Work team identification and team building

Doug wanted to write up the program as a case study and needed a name for the program. "Human Relations Training" wasn't right. Neither was "Leadership Training," although that was one of the activities. "Management Development" was not appropriate because the program involved the whole organization. "Organization Improvement" was too bland, so we named it "Organization Development." Change was in the air.

Developing the Managerial Grid

By pure coincidence, and during the same time frame, Herb Shepard and Robert Blake were conducting an organizationwide change program at the Bayway, New Jersey plant of Esso (now Exxon). The intervention was a series of workshops using a method that Blake and Jane Srygley Mouton had recently developed called the *managerial grid*. The entire management group at the Bayway refinery attended one-week workshops in which, using the grid method and

working in learning teams, they identified every member's management style, the style of the team, their intergroup effectiveness, and
their planning competence.

The grid was based on the theory that attitudes of managers in
large part determined their behavior. The basic concept was that
we all have some amount of concern for results and some amount
of concern for people. Using a nine-point scale, Blake and Mouton
located five positions on a grid, identifying five different styles based
on the mix of attitudes. For each position there were two numbers:
the first representing concern for results, the second concern for
people. If one had high concern for results and low concern for people, the style would be recorded as 9.1. If one had high concern for
people and low concern for results the style was 1.9. Low concern
for both was 1.1, moderate concern for both was 5.5. The "hero" of
the model was 9.9—high concern for both results and people.

Many organizations adopted the managerial grid program as a
way of developing appropriate attitudes and styles in their people.
The purpose of these programs was to effect a change in the culture
and way of work for the managers and workers. Eventually, the
Blake-Mouton Managerial Grid Program was widely adopted by
companies in the oil business. Consumer businesses, including the
engineering division of Procter & Gamble, also began to adopt it as
the basis for systemwide change programs.

I had recruited Bob Blake to co-train with me in a leadership
workshop I was conducting for YPO. In this workshop Blake
decided to add two phases to his four-phase grid program and to
name the six-phase program Grid Organization Development. We
tested the idea with the participants in the workshop, and it got
support. Blake asked if I was interested in joining up with him and
Jane Mouton in selling and conducting OD programs. It was a
tempting offer, but I decided to maintain my autonomy rather than
become identified with any particular set of tools and methods.
Blake graciously gave me a lifetime agreement to use the methodology, without paying him royalties.

Organization Development Versus Management Development

Organization development was emerging and developing quickly and, as it happened, none too soon. As part of the Great Society under President Lyndon Johnson, legislation was passed requiring mandatory retirement at the age of sixty-five for civil servants. These rules were adopted by most businesses. What no one had anticipated was that over 60 percent of the top managers of the major corporations would then have to retire in two or three years. Most organizations had no succession plans in place. Key people worked as long as they wanted to if they stayed healthy. Now organizations were facing a major loss of leaders, with relatively few systematic replacement plans. Organizations rushed to create succession lists for key jobs. But in many organizations, there had been little attention to coaching subordinates. Potential successors had minimum preparation for the role they might assume.

Top managements turned to the training departments to develop programs to address the problem—many times on a crash basis. Management development specialists came to the fore. This role tended to attract senior trainers, in part because the compensation was higher than the regular training roles. What management development specialists did was mostly training, since that is what they had done before. "Management development" became "manager development." The training focused on the same skills as supervisory training, but with more attention on team leadership.

By 1961, there were enough people involved in the field that the issue of how to differentiate organization development from management development was a live one. I was committed to the notion that OD was a systemwide change effort, whereas management development was really *manager development*, using training methods for awareness and skill development in managing people. I produced a definition as follows: *Organization development is a*

planned systemwide change program, using behavioral science knowledge,
to move the organization to a new "state."

The definition proved quite controversial for many OD practitioners. They had previously been human relations trainers and manager developers. Their work was heavily values-driven. They embraced such values as: individuals should always strive to reach their full potential as human beings; self-awareness is essential for personal development; good management of interpersonal relations is a core skill and required for working in groups (teams). Organization development activities focused on the personal development process and included self-awareness training, team building, intergroup relations workshops, and goal-setting workshops.

For many practitioners of organization development in organizations, the personal and group processes were the focus of attention. The outcomes/objectives were increased skills, not organization change. An effective program under their definition would increase individual and group effectiveness, without primary regard to the organization's goals. In contrast, the "organization" in my definition was the client system for organization development. My definition was from more of a cultural anthropologist's or sociologist's perspective. Interventions were change programs whose goal was to create a new culture, new ways of working, changed management style, a reward system congruent with cultural values, allocation of tasks, and roles to produce optimum use of its human resources.

There was a major gap in the two types of definitions. Some definitions were based on developmental psychology; I took a more cultural anthropological stance. An assumption underlying my definition was that the organization change effort toward a "new state" had to relate to the "business goals" of the organization's leadership. The central focus is on the organization and the change process; team and individual change are by-products. Controversial as it was, I made my definition known through articles, my first book in the OD series, speeches at OD network meetings, and training sessions at NTL and elsewhere.

Early Applications of Organization Development

A few organizations adopted the *personal growth model* as the basis for a culture change. One organization that chose this route and engaged in a massive and successful culture change effort was TRW Systems in Redondo Beach, California. When I first started consulting there the company was called Space Technology Laboratories (STL). It was on the leading edge of developing space vehicles and systems for the air force.

The culture of STL was unique. Sixty percent of the staff had Ph.D.s or other advanced degrees. When the company changed from a purely research group to a profit-making institution, Reuben Mettler, the CEO, determined to create a workplace culture that would support freedom to be innovative and creative with a minimum of bureaucratic rules and restrictions. He created a "campus" that housed their laboratories, manufacturing, and general office. The offices used an open design but with plenty of privacy for individuals. People were located near colleagues with whom they did regular work. Conference rooms and team rooms were created to ensure maximum access and optimum use. Training facilities were placed throughout the campus so each functional group would have its own space rather than having to use a centralized training facility. Support functions such as administration and human resources were located in the area that they supported. Only small functional groups were located together.

The vice president for industrial relations was a key figure in setting up the campus. He was also very committed to developing personnel policies and procedures that would support Mettler's philosophy and values. While keeping the oversight of the traditional personnel functions, he created a deputy function that would coordinate and lead the change effort. He appointed Sheldon Davis to fill this role. Davis had been a line worker and was moved to management in personnel. As part of his professional development he had obtained a Ph.D. in the Organization Behavior Program at

Case Western University. Herb Shepard, who headed this program, had been his mentor.

Shepard and Davis designed a process for managing the change effort. They decided that a critical success factor would be the behavior of the personnel staff, who were primarily traditional personnel types. Their responsibilities included compensation and benefits, recruitment and selection, technical and supervisory training, management development, and manpower planning. They were basically a service and monitoring function for corporate policies. They were not involved in organization improvement or change management or strategic planning.

The design of the change called for the development of new skills for the senior people in personnel. They needed to

- Learn consulting skills

- Be interpersonally competent

- Understand planned change

- Get comfortable with ambiguity, both in roles and functions

- Become facilitators of groups

- Become members of the line and staff management teams

These changes presented major challenges to the staff. Davis made it clear that if senior personnel people could not become competent in the new way of work, they had better look elsewhere. Jim Dunlop, the vice president, backed him up. Davis realized to get this amount of change within about a year required outside help. He and Shepard recruited a consulting team of top-level, applied behavioral scientist-practitioners, including Charles Ferguson, Robert Tannenbaum, Edgar Schein, and me.

Our team met quarterly for three days, first by ourselves, then with the internal people who had chosen to come on board the change effort. Reuben Mettler provided strong support for the effort. After a few meetings of the group, he joined up for half a day to hear about our efforts and results and to share issues he wanted us to address. Later as our insider-outsider team worked together, we would meet with the top management group at least twice a year. With Mettler's support, a number of interventions were initiated: all managers attended company workshops on individual development and team building; the appraisal systems were altered to focus on improvement planning; the work rules were modified to maximize individual freedom, including flexible work hours and casual dress.

By pushing the management styles envelope, TRW became a model for organizations trying to become more efficient and more human. There were plenty of quantifiable results on both counts. It became the industry leader in securing contracts from the air force and NASA. The relationship between bottom-line results and the culture in which work was done came to epitomize an effective company. Even today, thirty years later, it is held up as a model of sophisticated values and process-driven organization that, by supporting creativity, innovation, and individual potential, has created a highly profitable business and a fine place to work.

For me personally, the work with the team of inside and outside consulting partners influenced my future relationships with client organizations. I learned that an inside-outside partnership of change agents is the most effective structure for optimizing the talents of both in supporting organization change.

Patterns of Practice

I now had participated in four organizationwide change efforts: the General Mills Bottoms Up Management Program, the HCA organization development effort, the Raymond Organization

Development Program, and the STL/TRW Program. I had found some patterns in my work. For an organization development program to happen, the following factors were necessary:

- There had to be an identified need for major change.

- The top of the organization had to want the change and have a high commitment to investing the time and resources to reach their desired change goals.

- The key leadership had to have at least a moderate degree of readiness to use help in implementing the change effort.

I was also finding that in the relationship I needed to play several different roles. I would function as an expert in activities such as conducting a team-building effort of a training activity or a communications-improvement intervention. On many problems I would be a consultant, working with clients to help them increase their capacity to resolve the issues on which we were working. I was an educator: I linked and transferred outside knowledge and experience and theories to help the client work the issues. I was a counselor. Inevitably, if we were working on a long-term or powerful change effort, we would develop a more trusting relationship over time. From the original dependency on my expertise on the organization issues, there would often arise a need for some personal counseling. This was particularly true in working with family businesses. I learned that it was essential to have boundaries and criteria about when to perform the various roles. A major tension was how to balance professional and personal relationships with clients. This took some practice.

By the mid-sixties, the organization development function was widely recognized as part of the personnel or human resource management department in organizations. The title Organization Development Specialist appeared in tables of organization and salary schedules. The role was most often filled by people who previously had been in the training or management development function and who wished to broaden their client base to teams and total organizations. Their contributions moved from training events such as team-building workshops and off-sites, to consulting with executives on organization design, career planning, reward systems, and development strategies.

Most line managers still perceived the function as "soft side" training and development. As the OD contribution became seen as more helpful, progressive managers began using the OD staff as their personal consultants. By the late sixties, a number of practitioners saw increased opportunities as external consultants and began creating their own consulting businesses.

A Network Forms

In 1967, Herb Shepard and Shel Davis convened a group of senior OD practitioners at Bethel to explore the possibilities of creating a "professional/educational" mechanism for sharing experience and learning from each other. The group rejected the idea of a formal organization or association and opted for a "network"—a loosely organized group of people who wanted to meet periodically for their own fun and professional development. Warner Burke, who was staff head of the OD Division of NTL, convinced the NTL board to endorse and sponsor the network. He became its first executive director, thus ensuring some sort of infrastructure.

From that humble beginning, the network has grown and developed. It was incorporated in New Jersey in 1977 and, as of 1997, has approximately 3,300 members and a professional staff. Their annual conference in 1996 had nine hundred attendees. The 1997 conference, entitled "Advancing OD Practices amidst Paradox" will be attended by close to one thousand practitioners. There is a national publication, *The OD Practitioner*, published four times a year. There are a number of very active regional and semiautonomous local chapters. Several of the regional groups have publications of their own; the most prominent is San Francisco's *Bay Area OD Network*. In the brief space of thirty years, the network has grown from a volunteer-owned and volunteer-managed enterprise to a professional association.

Codifying the Field

By 1967 there were over a hundred OD practitioners. Some articles describing the field had appeared in journals and magazines, mostly in the *Journal of Applied Behavioral Science*, an NTL publication. There was no overall description of the field.

When Douglas McGregor died suddenly in 1964, he left behind a partially completed manuscript of a book on which he had been working for several years. His widow, Caroline, asked Edgar Schein, Warren Bennis, and me to finish the book. We were all involved in our teaching and research, and we each had a consulting practice in organization change or development—and we agreed to Caroline's request. After finishing Doug's book, we decided to create a series of books that would describe the state of the OD field. Warren would write one on the philosophy and theory behind OD. Ed would write one on process consultation. They persuaded me to write one on the state of practice in OD. I had not written since my earlier book on managing workshops in 1950, but I agreed to try.

To fill out an overview of the field, we asked Richard Walton, a Harvard professor, to write a book on third-party consultation, in which he had done a lot of research. Paul Lawrence and Jay Lorsch agreed to write about differentiation and integration, a major conceptual contribution to understanding organization behavior. Robert Blake and Jane Mouton agreed to do a book on the Managerial Grid Program, their very popular organizationwide training and organization development program.

I conceived the idea of packaging the books as six books in a box. We tried to get a publisher. McGraw-Hill and Prentice Hall, the most logical companies, turned us down. Luckily, we found

Richard Fenton, an ex-McGraw-Hill editor, who had recently joined Addison-Wesley, a small publishing house in Reading, Mass. He became an enthusiastic and creative collaborator and convinced Addison-Wesley management to publish the six books. Thus was the Addison-Wesley OD series born. Today, thirty years later, there are thirty-five titles in the series, which is still alive and well. Schein and I are the series editors; Bennis withdrew since he was a consulting editor for another publisher.

Training for Professionals in Organization Development

The OD network provided a mechanism for professional interaction and development, but there was no professional training for OD practitioners. At the time (1966–67), NTL had a policy that senior fellows could offer to conduct programs at Bethel. If the board approved, NTL would include it in the summer program.

I had been teaching a course on change at MIT for several years. I had also continued to staff NTL labs. I felt there was a market for experienced OD practitioners to engage in a training program in OD methods, practice, and concepts.

Program for Specialists in Organization Development

I designed a four-week program. The first week would be focused on learning theory and on individual and group dynamics (a requirement for admission was previous participation in a basic NTL lab). The second week would focus on consulting skills and the change process. The third and fourth weeks would focus on change theory, large system dynamics, and intervention theory. Participants would engage in a number of case practices. They would be organized into four learning teams, which would be their "home room" for the program. This also required a core staff of four.

In the design, the first week was led by the core staff. In the second and third weeks, we would add an adjunct faculty—a big name in the field—with expertise in the content of that week. Our adjuncts included Herb Shepard, Chris Argyris, and Sheldon Davis the first year. In the second year, Warren Schmidt and I were co-deans. The other core staff were Warner Burke and Harvey Hornstein.

The program, called PSOD (Program for Specialists in Organization Development), was a success from the first. There was an ever-increasing market of OD practitioners who welcomed the chance to participate in a focused "learning experience." It was "graduate school" for many OD practitioners and continues to this day. With roughly twenty-four people a year, this amounts to over seven hundred practitioners having gone through the training.

Other Professional Training Programs

Growing out of the success of PSOD, several other programs emerged. Harvey Hornstein and Warner Burke were joined by Noel Tichy (all of whom taught at Columbia University) to create a program using a similar conceptual and learning group framework. Billie Alban, who had attended the second PSOD, joined them in conducting the program, now called ODHRM (for Organization Development Human Resource Management). The program is still given annually and is always sold out. It is limited to forty participants and quickly has a long waiting list for the following year.

The first degree program also was heavily influenced by PSOD and laboratory training, California-style. Pat Williams, who was teaching at San Jose State University in California, and David Peters, a graduate of our program at MIT, and then faculty in the business school of Pepperdine University, created a two-year master's program at Pepperdine, called the Master's in Science in Organization Development (MSOD).

The first course started in 1975; I first taught in it during 1976. In the summer of 1995, I attended the twentieth reunion of participants in the program. Almost one hundred people attended from the twenty classes. Bob Tannenbaum and I were invited guests.

Both of us had been staff or faculty in the program, Bob for twenty years and I for nineteen. That was a memorable weekend, with a wonderful group of people, who were now successful in their careers.

In addition to helping with the design of both the Columbia and Pepperdine programs, I have taught in them since their inception. It is one of the highlights of my year to spend a day or two with these very committed mid-career practitioners. They are hungry to learn, secure in themselves, and a joy to work with.

In the eighties, NTL started a degree program in conjunction with American University. Edith and Charles Seashore founded the program, which is a two-year design with a slightly different format. Participants spend two two-week sessions at Bethel and a number of long weekends over the course of the program.

Progress and Learning

By the end of the decade, my professional life was threefold: teaching, writing, and consulting. I was teaching organization behavior in the Sloan School of Management at MIT. I had written one book on OD and was co-editing the Addison-Wesley OD series with Bennis and Schein. I had several organization clients with whom I worked on a regular basis.

In the United States I had an ongoing relationship with P&G manufacturing. I had consulted with General Foods, Sherwin Williams, and several other companies. I had two major clients in Europe: J. Lyons and Imperial Chemical Industries (ICI). I made six trips to Europe each year, during the school holidays, during the month between semesters, and after school ended in May and before it started in September. During the slice of summer in between, I continued to live in Maine and to participate in one or two weeks of workshops at NTL in Bethel.

My European experience was a tough school. I made so many faux pas that I once considered writing an article about them. I learned and continued to learn about working in other cultures. By

1970 I had established parallel ongoing relationships in several countries. I was spending so much time in London that I decided to leave what I called my London wardrobe—suits that I would never wear in the United States—there. I stored a hanging bag with three suits and a suitcase with some shirts and other articles. I still follow the practice. It has always been affirming for me to arrive at my hotel in London, Amsterdam, or Copenhagen and have the concierge say, "Welcome back," or even, "Welcome home."

6

Working in Other Cultures

The NTL team that conducted leadership training in Austria in 1954 and trained Austrian professionals to conduct such training was an anomaly at that time. The United States had been relatively isolated from the rest of the world culturally, but international trade was booming and there were changes ahead. The NTL team was responsible for a change in attitude by some senior foreign aid officials. These officials sponsored a trip, during which applied behavioral scientists from nine countries visited NTL and other training centers. A revolution in communication and contact between countries had begun.

Leadership Training in the Netherlands

In 1956, when Marjan Schroeder visited NTL and we became good friends, she was contemplating starting an NTL-like program in the Netherlands. She was head of the social work department in the Netherlands Institute of Preventive Medicine of the National Health Service. Her department was responsible for leadership training.

We had several discussions about how to proceed with her ideas. She decided that for a first event she would invite two NTL trainers, Joseph Luft and Paul Buchanan, to conduct a program for a small group of her colleagues. That was successful. The following year she and a number of colleagues conducted a two-week program for leaders in the public and private sectors. Matt Miles, Jan Clee, and I were the trainers of the three learning groups. Marjan and two other professionals served as co-trainers, with an eye to conducting their own program the following year.

The next year these co-trainers conducted a two-week program for a similar group of leaders. Schroeder and the other co-trainers recruited me to consult with the staff, to work with them at staff meetings and clinics that year. The program was conducted in Dutch, and the staff meetings were to be in English to accommodate me. After the first meeting, in which everyone was struggling to work and plan in a second language, I suggested that they use Dutch and teach me a number of "jargon" words. I could listen to the "music" and intervene when I felt it appropriate.

My previous experience in Austria, where I had found I could communicate with the participants in the T-group even when they were speaking German, which I did not, helped me tremendously in cross-cultural listening. The experience is similar to visiting a friend, say in Paris, when you have only "book" French. You can communicate by asking, "How do you say?" It's far from perfect, but it's functional. Similarly, I could function in my role as consultant to the training staff.

The staff group became close friends as well as professional colleagues. They decided to set up a professional training association and be its founding members. The focus was on professional development. Every month they would meet on a Saturday for a seminar. (Although they were located all over the country, they could get to a meeting in an hour's time thanks to the small size of the country and its incredibly efficient national rail system.) They scheduled quarterly two-day workshops, at which they would bring in a senior staff person from NTL. Matt Miles, Warren Bennis, and I each conducted one.

In the summer following the first year, they scheduled a two-week training of trainers workshop, which Matt Miles and I conducted in a town called Petersburg in northern Holland. A couple of consultants and trainers from Denmark asked to be invited and were accepted as participants in this workshop.

In the second year of their planned two-year program, they developed criteria for a professional trainer. They developed a peer evaluation system in which each member was evaluated by the whole group. Those who met the criteria were then certified as human relations leadership trainers—a professional role that was recognized by the state. They also started a training program for the next generation of trainers. They made Matt Miles and me honorary members of the Dutch Training Association.

My trips to Holland soon generated other activities. Freddie Jeppeson, a senior vice president of BP Denmark, had participated in my first senior executive program at MIT in 1963. He was then president of the Danish Employers Association and arranged for my invitation to give a lecture to his association later that summer. He offered the large meeting room at BP headquarters as a venue for the event.

A Lecture in Distress

The chairman of the planning committee contacted me a few days before the scheduled date and asked that I arrive at three for my four o'clock lecture. I thought he wanted me there early in order to meet him and to check out the room and the facilities. I arrived to find the room set up for two hundred people in theater-style seating. At the end of the room was a bar and buffet. People began arriving at the same time I got there. They obviously knew the form and headed straight for the drinks.

By the time we moved to seats at four o'clock, these very formal, dark-suited managers were mostly asleep from an hour of heavy imbibing. The chairman of the association started to introduce me, in Danish. What I thought would be a two-minute introduction turned into a ten-minute biography. By then those who had stayed awake were now at least half asleep.

I was in a panic. Here I was, the visiting "professor." I was to give a talk for at least thirty minutes, in English (which, I had been told, the attendees all understood). But now they had just enjoyed a fine repast, were half awake, and probably disinterested at best. What could I say that would make any sense? I had a pretty good set of remarks prepared. I realized that I had nothing to lose, whether they liked it or not. I thanked the chairman and apologized for not being able to speak Danish. Drawing on experience from my meetings work fifteen years earlier, I told them that before I started my remarks I wanted to hear what they felt were their issues in managing change (the announced subject of the talk). In order to get everyone's ideas quickly, they should get into small groups. I had every other row turn their chairs around and talk, in Danish, with five or six people. I promised I would then sample the findings from the groups and try to make my remarks relevant to their issues. I started moving around the hall, putting people in groups, getting them to turn around.

The audience was in total shock. I had violated every expectation. Now they had to stay awake. Out of adversity sometimes comes innovation. The lecture was a big success, I'm sure more because of the shock of what went before than the content of my lecture.

Change Management in Denmark and Finland

While in Denmark, I visited with Hanne Ernst and her senior partner, Gunnar Hjelholt, who was engaged in some fascinating applied behavioral science projects. In the field of social change, Gunnar was a major force, influencing applied behavioral scientists all over the world. He was an innovator with great talent and strong values. His values were humanistic, his politics socialist; he was not accepted by the establishment. Gunnar and I had liked each other when we first met at Bethel, where he had been a visiting staff member; our experience together that summer deepened our friendship. His integrity, his willingness to stand up for his convictions (even those that were unpopular), his commitment to helping people learn and develop versus teaching them had considerable influence on my values and practice and my future professional behavior.

Gunnar had developed a four-week residential program for social sector leaders to help them understand community building and diversity through an experiential workshop. He and Hanne proposed that we set up and jointly conduct an NTL-type workshop for organization leaders. He had the location, a compound in the forest in southern Sweden, where he conducted his community workshops. We did one workshop and, based on the feedback, decided to do another the following year.

One of the participants at this second program was Lauri Penti, who was a member of the staff of the Finnish Management Institute (called LIFIM for its Finnish name), Finland's National Management Training Center. He invited me to do a workshop for senior managers on change management. That was the first of several visits to Finland and to LIFIM. Through this work in Finland, I learned much about the need to adjust one's content and contributions in a different culture. And, on the most basic level, since I had to work with translations, I learned still more about the importance of language in defining the culture.

Consulting in England

My experiences in the Netherlands expanded. And my consulting business grew and changed. In time, some of my stateside connections resulted in consulting work for me in England.

Hotel Corporation of America—in London

In 1962, I had my first consulting assignment in England. I was asked to work with the start-up management team for a hotel that Hotel Corporation of America (HCA), my client, was opening in London. I had worked with several such teams in the States but, as

I soon discovered, that was not the perfect preparation for this assignment.

My understanding of working in different cultures was sorely tested during the start-up days. The general manager, who was Austrian, was a terror to his subordinates and more than slightly paranoid. Management and staff consistently pointed out to me the terrible effects of his behavior. Yet when I suggested that we bring up their concerns at the team meetings, they refused to let them be surfaced. No matter how strong the negative feelings, it was not "correct" in British culture to publicly confront or give negative feedback to the boss. I was not able to break through this norm.

After the hotel opened, Roger Sonnabend assigned me to continue to work with the management team. The general manager did not want my services or my presence, but he couldn't fire me because I was there at the request of the owners of the company. I represented the threat of supervision by American managers, limits to his desired total authority. He continued to resent me, but we were able to work around him and not destroy the morale of the staff. After about a year, he was fired, and I worked with his replacement. Then, the team consulting worked fine.

More Family Business—Overseas

Another client of mine in New York was David Levit, president of DCA Industries, the former Doughnut Corporation of America. I had met David in YPO, and he had retained me to work with him as head of his company, which was a family business. His company was a principal supplier for the Bakery Division of J. Lyons Ltd., a family-owned billion-dollar catering, restaurant, and hotel conglomerate. In addition to restaurants, the famed Lyons Corner Houses, Lyons's major businesses included catering, hotels, ice cream, breads, and bakeries; it even extended into transportation and computer businesses.

David had suggested that I might want to meet Brian Salmon, his customer and a member of the owning family, with the hope that some consulting work might emerge. A few months later I received a call from a Mr. Brian Salmon. He mentioned David's referral and said he would very much like to meet "the professor." Would I please come and have tea with him?

We made a date. He told me how to get to his office in a taxi and said that a "commissionaire" would meet me there. I had no idea what a commissionaire was and didn't dare ask. When I arrived at the address, the taxi was waved into the "admin" block (what Americans would call the administration building) in the middle of a giant factory complex. The taxi stopped and I was met by a man in full uniform. He saluted and said, "Professor Beckhard? Please follow me!" We walked into a small lobby and to the lift (elevator). I noted he had six stripes on his arm patch. I thought he must be a general, at least. At the lift he turned me over to a corporal—two stripes—who was at least sixty years old. This man accompanied me in the lift to the fourth floor. Waiting there was a four-striper. I was handed over to him. Without saying a word he marched off; I was behind him, and proceeded down a quiet, car-peted hall past a number of closed doors of beautiful oak. We arrived at the proper door; he knocked, opened the door, and announced, "Professor Beckhard!" By then I was totally humbled. (It was only later I learned that retired military noncommissioned officers were often hired as doormen and ushers by companies and hotels. They were allowed to wear their military uniforms and medals. Hence my impressive escort.)

We entered a small, elegantly furnished office. A fiftyish, very distinguished looking, gray-haired gentleman dressed in a beautiful pin-stripe suit rose to greet me. He introduced himself and motioned me to sit down opposite him at his desk. There was another man, apparently a staff person. On the desk was an obvi-ously unread copy of my colleague Doug McGregor's book, *The Human Side of Enterprise*. Salmon introduced Geoffrey Mills, head of management development. That explained why the book was there.

From that beginning, Salmon asked me to consult with him on some issues in the bakery division. My next assignment was to help him with the consequences of a radical management decision he was contemplating. In an organization modeled after the Rothschild bank and the royal family—only family members could hold top positions—he was planning to promote a non-family member to a general manager's position. It had never been done. But Brian had convinced his siblings and elders that this change in promotion policy was necessary for the business: the third generation of the owning families was not yet ready to assume such responsibilities.

My experience with working with family businesses allowed me to help him through what turned out to be a horrendously difficult change. I was working in a totally strange culture. It was British, and that was different enough. It was a dynasty, a family empire. It was also a prominent Jewish family in Britain.

I quickly recognized some limitations in how I could help. I suggested they retain Harold Bridger, a distinguished consultant/researcher in the Tavistock Institute of Applied Behavioral Science, to work with the three generations of the Salmon family, the owners. Harold Bridger was a well-known consultant-scientist. He had known several of the family members in other settings. In addition to his professional credentials, Bridger was Jewish and would be accepted as understanding that culture. I suggested that I continue to work with Salmon and the bakery division management. Salmon was a wise man and a true gentleman; I enjoyed working with him and we became friends. He introduced me to his brother Neal, who was to be the next chief executive officer. Brian was to take on the role of chairman—the family leader and liaison to the business. I worked with the two brothers and with the personnel department for several years, visiting them three or four times a year.

A Division in Trouble

Some time after the change in promotion policy, the bakery division found itself in trouble: loss of market share and loss of competitive advantage put its survival at risk. The general manager was under fire, and there was little energy below the top group for any major change effort. The general manager had hired a major consulting firm, who had done a massive study and recommended a few structural changes. Not much had happened as a result. To cope with this emergency, I created the confrontation meeting.

The Confrontation Meeting

We had limited time. We wanted to disrupt people's schedules as little as possible, and we knew that I couldn't stay in London long. From earlier work, I had learned about the hourglass theory of energy: under stress, individuals or organization systems experience high negative energy. Because energy is "neutral," you can reduce stress by quickly converting the energy direction from negative to positive. Then the negative energy becomes an asset. The challenge is to turn the energy 180 degrees in the opposite direction. The best action is not to cool the energy by working on the morale and discomfort but to create some short-term goals that must be met.

We needed activity toward positive action. I designed a five-hour meeting in which the entire organization, about 110 people, could convene in one room for an entire day. They met first in heterogeneous groups to identify the blocks to freeing up the energy of the workforce and significantly increasing effectiveness. The group's output was listed on flip charts and pasted on the walls; there was no group consensus.

As meeting process manager and leader, I developed some categories such as decision-making and communication issues. In plenary session we assigned each item to a category. Then for ninety minutes, we worked in groups; the tasks were to select four or five items from the entire list that group members themselves could do something about. They were to prepare a short-term action plan of "promises" that they would share publicly. Their second task was to select from the whole list one or two items on which they wanted top management to take urgent action.

Each group reported about its promises. After reviewing the top management request list, the general manager commented on the items and indicated actions to be taken. The meeting was a great success. The whole organization became energized, productivity increased, and morale jumped. Yet in a visit three months later, I found that the initial energy had quieted down considerably. Life and work were better than before, but the energy for continued improvement was not high. The tension had not been maintained.

Confrontation, with Follow-Up

Several months later I conducted a similar meeting for another client. At the end, after the feedback, I got the manager to announce a follow-up two-hour meeting six weeks hence, at which he would report on actions the top team had taken, and he would receive similar reports from the work groups. That made all the difference in results. By adding in the need to review results, everyone was motivated to hold to their promises.

My article on the confrontation meeting was published in the March-April 1967 issue of the *Harvard Business Review*. Many companies use the technique. It is particularly in demand today, when there is much attention to new techniques of having problem-solving meetings with everyone in the room.

Working with Imperial Chemical Industries

Soon after I met Geoffrey Gilbertson, the personnel director of Imperial Chemical Industries' (ICI) agricultural division, he invited me to visit his organization and perhaps consult with him on some issues. Gilbertson was a remarkable man. He was in a wheelchair, with no use of his legs, due to early polio. He was both passionate and compassionate. Given an idea he believed in, he couldn't be stopped. His behavior often produced great frustration among more orthodox managers but, all had to admit, he got things done. His was probably the single greatest contribution to the health of ICI in the thirty years I worked with them.

Gilbertson had excellent skills and experience in industrial relations. He also had some strong points of view. He believed that it should be possible to find ways for unions and managements to collaborate on improving conditions in the workplace, even though their institutions were basically adversarial. He had established good personal relations with the union leaders in his area and with many national leaders.

Gilbertson was an avid learner. He had heard of Douglas McGregor and had visited him at MIT, where I first met him. He subsequently invited McGregor to do a consult with his board. He later invited Hollis Peter, who was then at the University of Michigan and has since retired to Australia, and Edgar Schein, a colleague of Doug's and mine, to make similar visits.

Because I was faculty adviser to an intern, Douglas Brynildson, who had been placed in ICI as part of a six-month internship with an ongoing organization development program, I had a fair amount of contact with Gilbertson. When he discovered that I was another colleague of McGregor's, he asked me to spend a couple of days meeting with his board and doing a diagnosis of an intergroup issue between the engineering and manufacturing divisions.

The brief luncheon meeting with the board went extremely well. The chairman asked me to come back and do some further consulting with the board. My work with them was seen as helpful. Gilbertson tried to refer me to another division board, which was in no mood for a consultant. But a couple of years later, in 1966, I did become a consultant to another division board. John Harvey Jones was deputy chairman of the heavy chemicals division, also located in the northeast of England. He was a visiting member of the agriculture division board and asked if I would do some work with his board. Although there were some mixed feelings from his chairman, he agreed to let me guide a team offsite with the heavy chemicals board. Thus developed a long-term relationship with that division, and an even longer-term relationship with John Harvey Jones.

A few years later, Geoffrey Gilbertson moved to the company headquarters in London to become an assistant general manager in the central personnel division. The general manager, Jack Coates, was an expert on international personnel management. The existing assistant, Donald Mumford, was experienced in working with senior management succession and development. So much of the work was with the union that they needed someone to head the industrial relations work. When Gilbertson moved from personnel to the headquarters staff, he arranged for me to consult with the new management team—Gilbertson, Coates, and Mumford—on their own functioning.

Interacting with the Unions

The unions were national; their contracts were negotiated every year. ICI had a relatively progressive consultation relationship with the unions, in which the union leadership was kept informed about the company in the context of a naturally adversarial relationship. In the mid-sixties, Great Britain had a labor government, which was basically controlled by the unions. It was a socialist democracy. Economically, the country was in terrible shape. Productivity per worker in industry was less than half that of Germany or the United States. All the major U.K. companies were installing productivity schemes to try to increase the motivation and productivity of their workers. Many of these schemes were hampered by laws that prohibited companies from giving raises to union members beyond the annual contract agreement without government permission.

Gilbertson wasn't interested in business as usual, and he devised a brilliant scheme for working around the legislation. He sold his scheme, called MUPS (Manpower Utilization and Payment Structure), to his management. Because the union leadership trusted him, they agreed to experiment with the scheme. Together the union leadership and Gilbertson convinced the government bureau-crats to give the scheme a try.

Gilbertson believed nonofficial, trusting relationships were essential if productivity was to be ensured. A basic assumption behind the scheme built on this belief: only through collaboration between workers on the site and first-line management on the site could you get the worker effort that would increase productivity. Gilbertson knew that the union would expect workers to be finan-cially rewarded for any increase they helped provide. After much work, he finally convinced ICI top management to accept this prob-ability, even if it meant initial additional costs to the company. He convinced them that management would have to give something up front if they wanted the union leadership to trust the process. Under the MUPS process, if the union stewards and the first-line management on a site agreed to sit down together to explore ways of increasing efficiency and productivity, with the assurance that no one would lose their job, the union members on that site would receive a one-time 15 percent bump in base pay, regardless of the contract agreement.

Gilbertson thought productivity probably would be increased between 15 and 20 percent, which would provide significant cost savings for the company in overtime alone. The program was installed in fourteen test sites. In the first year it produced a 22 per-cent increase in productivity, which significantly affected the bot-tom line. It also produced a new spirit of collaboration between workers and management. People felt more like partners than adversaries. When the company expanded the sites, similar out-comes occurred.

Staff Development

One of the consequences of the success of the MUPS process was the creation of inequities between union and nonunion employees. The large white-collar administrative and technical staff did not receive the MUPS raises. To combat this condition, under Gilbertson's leadership the company created a Staff Development Program (SDP). I advised on the process and worked personally with some division boards and the central office department to facilitate the process.

Every unit in the company, unions excepted, was asked to develop the criteria against which they wanted their performance to be measured. Against these criteria, they were to assess the present level of performance on a 1–5 scale. They were then to set the goal for their performance for one year ahead, when the program would end. If, for example, they were now at 3, their improvement goal might be anywhere from 3.5 to 5, the top. This goal became a promise to which the group was committed. The group was to present their goals to upper management, who would either approve or suggest lowering expectations if the goals were too ambitious, or send them back to raise the goals. If a group completed the process and received upper-management approval, the first ten levels in the pay site (administrators and technicians) would receive a one-time 15 percent raise; upper management would not. The savings in the first year came to five million pounds.

Training Managers to Manage the Change

In the MUPS program, first-line supervisors needed a lot of training to learn the skills of participating in joint consultations with their workers. Doug Brynildon, the intern, was assigned to head that program. Staff managers were trained to conduct the supervisory training.

In SDP, the problem was much more complex. The program required supervisors and section and department heads to lead discussions with their workers in small groups, an activity for which they had no preparation and low skills. They cried for help in how to run groups and how to manage a change effort. Bruce Neale, former personnel general manager under Gilbertson, had attended the second PSOD session at Bethel in 1968. He joined the central staff as project manager for a program to provide skill training to staff from personnel and other departments who were being assigned to help the supervisors develop the skills needed.

I was asked to put together a program. Together with Neale and another personnel staff supervisor, Arthur Johnston, we created a four-week program, based on the PSOD design, to help prepare supervisors to carry out the process. I recruited a staff from the United States and Europe. The program was traumatic for the staff. The Americans were comfortable with techniques such as the T-group or skills groups. The Europeans were more concerned with the substance of change, the dynamics of resistance, and managing diversity. To try to weld this group with diverse priorities into a faculty team was one of the most difficult challenges I faced in my professional career. I must admit that I did not get an A for my effort, although we managed, as professionals, to get a functional working relationship established. The attendees came out ahead: the program was effective in creating a cadre of change agents for ICI, who became a company resource in facilitating change.

In my thirty-year relationship with ICI, I consulted with six chairmen and their executive boards. (There was no CEO. The chairman, always an executive, was the de facto CEO. The board consisted of executive members, who were the top management team, and outside directors.) Each of the nine divisions or businesses of ICI was a multi-million-dollar enterprise; each operated semiautonomously. For the first fifteen years, my primary client was the personnel department, where I consulted on management training, succession planning, and organization design and change. In addition to consulting with the top team, I worked with Gilbertson and his colleagues on the development of the staff development program. As part of my work with the top personnel staff, I began working with Roland Wright, who later became chairman. I consulted with him and with his successor, Maurice Hodgson. The next chairman was John Harvey Jones, with whom I had a long and successful relationship. I worked with his successor, Denys

Hendersen, on the transfer of leadership and then until 1993, when ICI split into two companies. My last meeting with Hendersen was exactly thirty years after I had started working with ICI.

Consultant and Teacher

In this, as with my other experiences, I learned that as a consultant I could only add value and that I must be explicit with myself and the client as to what value I did add. I also realized that my most significant interventions were educational, whether teaching change courses or consulting with senior managers and helping them develop concepts. And so, I found myself in the role of the teacher.

7

Teaching—and Learning

Another life-defining event occurred in the spring of 1963. I was making a presentation at a chapter meeting of the Society for the Advancement of Management (SAM) in Cincinnati. Doug McGregor was speaking on the same program. We had been recruited by the chapter president, Nick Lunken, with whom we had both served on the NTL board. Doug and I both had made arrangements to fly out on evening planes—he back to Boston to teach the next day and I to a consulting assignment in New York. A horrendous snowstorm hit Cincinnati, and we were grounded. After the meeting we rushed to the railroad station and caught a ten o'clock train for New York. There were no sleeper cars available so we sat up most of the night talking, sharing where we were in life. Doug had recently returned to MIT from a stint as president of Antioch College. I had a full consulting agenda and was conducting workshops using my change model. I had taught a course at Teachers College, Columbia University, the previous semester, when Ken Herrold needed a substitute during his sabbatical.

Doug was building a team of young faculty to support him in a new department of organization studies. He had recruited two brilliant young Ph.D.s, Warren Bennis from Boston College and Ed Schein from Harvard. In the middle of the night, he suddenly asked me if I would be interested in joining his team for at least a semester as a lecturer. I would teach one course on change. He said he thought the organization studies group would be stronger by adding a practitioner who worked in the real world to help balance the very academically oriented Schein and Bennis. McGregor himself had a foot in both camps as teacher-consultant.

I had never thought of joining academia; however, the opportunity to work with McGregor and his colleagues was irresistible. I agreed. After a year's teaching (and after considerable pressure from Doug), Howard Johnson, then dean of the school, made an exception to his rule of not renewing lecturers' one-year contracts. I was appointed lecturer for another year, then a senior lecturer for several years, then adjunct (half-time) full professor for ten years. In all, that first commitment stretched into twenty-one years on the faculty.

Teaching at MIT was a daunting challenge. The students were brilliant and sophisticated. The faculty were the best in the business. What could I bring to the party? Luckily, I had learned a great deal from my association with NTL, both in theory and concepts, and from my exposure to great minds in the field.

Teaching About Learning

I had already used the practicum model, with live cases, in an NTL workshop that focused on designing and facilitating change in large systems. I had also used this model in various professional development settings. Now it was time to apply it in a different venue.

Learning to Teach

But first I had to develop a course plan, which I had never done before. With the help of my colleagues, I devised a one-semester course using inductive learning methods. I created a content theme for each session. I organized the class into small learning teams of three or four students. Each student would have two overlapping memberships—one on a learning team and one in a class.

The system required that I give grades, but how would I determine a grade in this subject? I could circumvent the system, giving each student a pass or a fail. That would satisfy the system but not the students. In the highly competitive environment of MIT, students wanted specific grades.

I knew nothing about grading students, and no one was able to give me much guidance. In pondering my dilemma, I recalled the best class I had ever attended: it was during my first year at Pomona College. The course, taught by Everett Dean Martin, was entitled, "The Intellectual and Social History of the United States." The content covered the period from Plato and Aristotle to the present (then 1935). The design included three lectures a week from Dr. Martin; two meetings of a seminar group, for which we had to prepare papers for discussion; and writing a pensée—a thought paper on whatever each student chose that was to define some thoughts on the personal meaning of the course. This course had been one of the most difficult yet rewarding experiences of my college career.

Dr. Martin's grading system was as follows: half the grade was based on his evaluation of the quality of the pensée; one-quarter of the grade was from a peer and graduate assistant evaluation of the quality of work in the seminar; and one-quarter was for participation in the class sessions. Knowing little of the MIT grading culture, I set my requirements the same way. At the first session, I assigned the pensée and told the students my grading formula. Initially there were rumblings, but I wound up using this design in every course I taught.

Using the Pensée

Since there was to be no exam, the students initially thought the course would not be demanding, and it would be easy to get a good grade. But the pensées set up an interesting dynamic. In making the assignment, I explained that the paper could be on any subject. The universal title was, "The Meaning of the Course for Me." It could be any length—short, I hoped. What it could not be was a literature or book review, or a regurgitation of my lectures. Part of the criteria on which I would judge their work was that I had to find the "whole person" in the paper.

For years, every class went through the same process. At first, they thought writing the pensée would be so easy that they postponed work on it until just before it was due (halfway through the semester). As the due date got close, I would have office visits from a number of students trying to clarify what I wanted in the pensée. I would repeat my original instructions. This caused tremendous frustration in the quantitatively oriented students, most of whom were high achievers who couldn't tolerate anything less than an A. Since they realized the pensée was half the grade, they put in frantic all-night sessions before the due date to get the paper finished on time. (They knew that I would penalize them for late delivery unless they had a special excuse.)

Although writing the pensée was a traumatic experience for many students, the quality of many of the papers was wonderful. Beyond the grade, I commented on each pensée. Later, there was almost universal feedback that it had been an important learning experience. Alumni often recounted to me what it had meant to them. For me, the pensées themselves repeatedly reaffirmed my belief that given a chance, the potential for creativity and innovation and introspection in all of us will come out. They revealed the students' inner capacity to integrate, internalize, and innovate.

Establishing Goals for Learning

My teaching goal for that first course—and for many that came later—was to help the students understand enough about the learning process to use it in their mentoring, consulting, or teaching roles with their subordinates. Since all learning is a change process, the "rules" of change must apply. When you learn something you are different than you were before you learned it. You change. I defined five levels of change through learning

- Change in knowledge

- Change in understanding

- Change in attitude

- Change in behavior

- Change in skill

Each level assumes all the levels above it. For example, a change in attitude requires a change in knowledge and a change in understanding.

An issue for the teacher is determining what to accomplish in helping the student learn, that is, what the deepest level of change to occur with the students is. If the teacher wants change in knowledge (for example, the knowledge that two plus two equals four), the teacher has only to impart it, and the students have to remember it until the test. If change in understanding (the significance of the year 1492) is the goal, the teacher has to do more, as do the students if the transfer of understanding is to take place. They both have to spend more time on the interaction. If change in attitude (history isn't worth learning) is the goal, the teacher must realize that people cannot move from attitude A to attitude B directly; they must go through neutral first. To change attitudes, people must free themselves of their present attitude (bias) in order to be open to developing a new attitude. If change in behavior is the goal, another set of rules applies. First the learner must exhibit the present behavior. Next the learner must receive feedback on the gap between present behavior and the desired behavior. The learner must then experiment and possibly fail with the new behavior. After practicing the behavior in a safe setting, the learner can finally apply the behavior in real situations.

Golf is a good example. When I was in my forties, I decided to take some golf lessons. The required elements for learning were me, a golf club, and a golf ball. The pro asked me to hit a couple of balls (demonstrating present behavior). Then he told me what was necessary: a new and painful grip, a new stance, keeping my head down, and on went the list. He had me experiment with these changes and find my swing. Using a five iron, I experimented and failed; I modified my stance and tried again and again (experimenting). When I found a pattern that seemed to work, the pro had me practice over and over using that pattern or swing. By the end of a half-hour lesson, the shots were going beautifully. After a few practice lessons, the pro suggested that I walk over to the nearest tee and play a hole or two. I walked those few yards, set up, and hit the ball. Or tried. I couldn't apply what I'd just done so well in practice. The different setting (a good golfer offering some help, a foursome wanting to play through) changed everything. I knew what I was supposed to do, but I couldn't yet do it. The same principles apply in changing managerial or interpersonal style. It involves taking all of the steps and having time to practice them.

In my teaching, I would help the learners apply this change model to their own real-life work and relationships. My courses were popular, particularly with students who were going into consulting. MIT had a reciprocal arrangement with Harvard, allowing students from one school to take some courses in the other. About 30 percent of my students were from the schools of education, government, and business at Harvard. I always had to cut off the enrollment in order to allow priority for the MIT students, given the physical restrictions in the classroom.

The Change Practicum

For advanced students, I created a practicum that focused on consulting with clients on large system change. In designing it, I made several assumptions

- I wanted it to be an interactive design, in which students would apply the concepts as they were learning them

- I wanted students to have cases—preferably live cases in which they were involved—that they could use to apply the model. I realized this would be difficult for students who had no practical experience, so I created cases in which they could practice

- I wanted the sessions to add up to a model of change management

In this practicum, called Consulting and Large System Change, I used one aspect of my change model—diagnosing the present state—as the model. I used the Lippitt, Watson, Wesley book, *The Planning of Change* as a primary resource. I recruited current and former clients of mine to be "clients" to the student consulting teams. At the first session of class I posted the names of the clients and descriptions of their affiliations—president of a small company, daughter of the CEO of a large company who was being groomed for the top job, bishop of a diocese, personnel manager in a high-tech company, and so on. Class members signed up for the client they would like to consult. From this we created learning teams for each client. I gave each team their client's contact address and phone number; teams were to contact the client (who had already been primed to expect a call). The team had to learn about the client's organization and try to find what change problem the client wanted to present.

I suggested that the students take the clients to dinner the night before at a local hotel for a briefing on the client's problem to be presented the next day. I gave each team a budget of $100 for this purpose, thus raising some eyebrows in the controller's department. Fortunately we rarely needed the money; most of the clients picked up the dinner bill. The next morning the consulting team would present their client to the class and then start the consultation in the front of the room.

I made it very clear that the prime purpose of the consulting session was to provide learning about large system consulting and diagnosis for the class as a whole, not just for the consulting team. During the consultation, if I felt an intervention was appropriate, I would step in front of the players, stop the discussion, turn to the class, and ask a question such as, How do you think the client is feeling now? What strategy do you think the consultants are following? What do you think the consultants should do next? Class members would shout out responses. The entire consultation was videotaped.

At the end of ninety minutes, we would take a break. When we returned from break, the client and I would sit up front, and the consulting team would sit with the rest of the class. I would interview the client and try to assess the value of the consultation (for which we all imagined the client had paid a $100 fee). I would ask how much they felt the consultants helped, whether they got their money's worth, what they felt about the members of the consulting team (there were always two consultants). Sample client replies were, "I had trouble following the consultants' agenda" and "I had done some preparation for this meeting, but the consultants didn't seem to care about that." One frustrated client said, "If I were really paying for this, I would have thrown them out of my office in the first five minutes." Another said, "I felt I was there to help the consultants." Other, more positive comments included, "I got a couple of great ideas out of them. I have two things I'm going to work on right away," and "This made me think about some things in a different way. It was really helpful."

After the interview, the client would join me as a faculty, as the class "processed" the consultation and the learnings they had experienced. In a clinic mode we would discuss alternative strategies, pitfalls, and things to think about. Later, in the team's next meeting, they would review the videotape of the consulting session to pull learnings from the experience. By then, my teaching assistant and one member of the presenting team had watched and marked the tape as an aid to an analysis of the process. Often the interventions were discussed as learning points. Clients loved participating in the practicum, and the students had a useful, and usually stimulating, experience.

A Chapter Closes

My retirement from the Sloan School of MIT was to take effect at the end of the spring term of 1984. One day in February of that year, two of my closest colleagues, Edgar Schein and Edwin Nevis, took me to lunch, where they gave me an enormous gift. They had decided upon and gotten approval from the Sloan School to have a Richard Beckhard celebration. When they shared their plans with MIT's industrial liaison office, which conducted seminars for MIT alumni and friends, the director suggested making it an all-MIT Richard Beckhard Day. That office would sponsor a symposium for the day, and the Sloan School would give a dinner that evening.

I was flabbergasted. This was not standard practice either at Sloan or MIT. I still wonder how these two colleagues were able to get this to happen. They wanted me to take an active role in the design of the symposium and to have a major voice in selecting the speakers. I did not want this to be tribute to me; I wanted there to be real content. We agreed on a full-day design. In the morning there would be presentations by three clients with whom I had worked; they would talk about the development of their own organizations. In the afternoon three professional colleagues could talk about their work.

Ed Schein chaired the morning meeting. The speakers were John Harvey Jones, then chairman and CEO of Imperial Chemical Industries; Ivan Lansberg, founder and CEO of Grupo Lansberg, a group of forty or so insurance companies in Venezuela; and George Raymond, CEO and board chairman of the Raymond Company, a materials-handling manufacturing company with whom I had worked for over twenty years.

Ed Nevis chaired the afternoon session. The speakers were Warren Bennis, Rosabeth Moss Kanter, Shosanah Zuboff (a colleague from the Harvard Business School), and Robert Schrank (a long-time colleague and friend and the author of *Ten Thousand*

Working Days). Each of them talked about their current work and enthusiasms.

Over three hundred people attended the symposium: colleagues, students, and alumni; friends and family; several people from Europe. The gatherings at the coffee breaks were like alumni meetings. Old friends and acquaintances meeting again, people meeting others that they had wanted to meet. It was like a very extended family. At lunch, I had the special treat of sitting with a group of my former graduate students. After the symposium, there was a reception, at which I was able to wander around and talk to a number of friends and colleagues.

That evening, the Sloan School gave a dinner at the MIT faculty club for about fifty people. My friends Edgar Schein and Edwin Nevis had arranged a wonderful program. After bantering back and forth about me, they called on several people to make brief remarks. The first was Chris Argyris, who at that time was at the Harvard School of Education. He paid me the honor of saying I was the "best teacher at Harvard." It was a bit of an inside joke: MIT and Harvard had reciprocal arrangements, and he had sent a number of his students to take my classes. Marc Gerstein, a student whom I had mentored in both his master's and Ph.D. programs and who was a good friend, represented students. The third speaker was my wife, Elaine, who said some funny things about the personal part of my life. The final speaker was Abraham Siegel, the dean of the Sloan School. He made some nice remarks and then announced that the school had created a fund for the Richard Beckhard Prize, an annual award for the best article in my field; the article would be published in the *Sloan Management Review*. The first winner of the prize was Peter Senge.

The day and the announcement had me stunned. It was incredible. As I said in my remarks at the end of the day, I was the mechanism for a grand gathering of people with common interests and similar professional lives in academia, practice, or management. To be so honored—and while still alive—was beyond my experience or fondest dream. It was overwhelming, a day and honor I shall never forget.

Teaching Practitioners

During my teaching career, I was asked to do a workshop on change for a company management training program, so I condensed the model that I used in my MIT class into a one-day program called Using a Model in Managing Change; I have also developed a two-day, one-day, and half-day format. I continue to conduct an occasional workshop using the model. A number of colleagues use the model in one form or length in their own training and consulting.

In addition to my various teaching positions at MIT, over the years I had a contract as an education consultant to the Young Presidents Organization (YPO). The roots of the YPO were planted in the early fifties by Ray Hickock, the second-generation owner and president of the Hickock Belt Company in upstate New York. He contacted some of his friends in similar positions about getting together periodically to share some of their concerns: the loneliness of being on top, the need to learn what it's like to have final responsibility for both work and people, and so on. He suggested monthly seminars with guest experts and a social evening with spouses. Soon such groups sprang up in many areas due to the networks of business connections and friendships. In the mid-fifties, a national YPO was created. Membership was for presidents under forty whose companies grossed a certain dollar amount. In later years, when many of the original members turned fifty, two or three organizations were created for alumni of YPO.

In 1958, Bob Hood, who was then program chairman for the convention, retained me to help him with program design. I used some of my meetings skills to create a more participative workshop program, and the members liked it. I was asked to do the same thing in following years. In 1960, Roger Sonnabend, the chairman for that convention, came up with the concept of a *university for presidents;*

we redesigned the program. Under the new format there were over forty classes on a wide variety of subjects offered during the week. Experts in business management, cultural subjects, social subjects, and family dynamics gave mini-courses. In the 1962 convention, there were over sixty mini-courses offered during the week. The university concept became the basis for all future national meetings and continues to this day. As the organization got bigger, YPO added in regional universities and other learning activities, including seminars with business leaders across the world.

My consulting contract moved beyond the conventions to include advising on educational seminars. I also conducted, at their request, a series of one-week leadership workshops, based on the NTL program. These workshops were attended by over a hundred members in the period of a year.

Lessons from Teaching

The concept of joint inquiry was a basic element of both my practice and my teaching, whether of graduate students or practitioners. This was different from the traditional role of the teacher teaching and the students learning. I found that the idea of joint learning is very threatening to many teachers, but for me it was a much more satisfying process. In my experience, learning is best when it is a joint inquiry between teacher and student, in which both learn. In the areas I was teaching—skills, competencies, attitudes, and values—that was the only way the teaching-learning transaction could be effective. It was not like teaching arithmetic or history.

Amid all this teaching and doing, this was a very busy period of my life. What I needed was time to process my learnings, which were tremendous. Some of these learnings I transferred directly to the PSOD program at NTL, whose design I based on the MIT practicum. Some I used in my consulting. Soon, I would put my lessons and learnings to use in yet another forum.

8

Changing Large Systems Change

My learnings from my consulting and teaching were multifold. All that I was teaching and learning were tested in my professional life and career. My involvement with a major countrywide educational intervention let me give the change model a real test in action and become fully aware of the power of an educational intervention to effect fundamental and profound change.

Operaciones Desarollo in Colombia

Manual Carvajal was from Colombia and owned a large printing and publishing empire in Cali. He had decided to take a year off from his work to attend the Sloan Fellows Program—the year-long, prestigious master's program we conducted for mid-career executives. The program, which he took from 1963 to 1964, had quite an impact on him—one that he took back with him to Colombia. During discussions outside of class, he had shared with us tales of the horrible conditions in his country and his passionate desire to do something about them. He realized that if there was any hope for Colombia changing from a backward Third World country to at least a civil society with some economic base and a place where leadership pays attention to social need, it would be up to the private sector to initiate an effort to get there.

In Cali at that time, there was 95 percent unemployment. Fifty-one percent of the people had never seen money as a medium of exchange; life expectancy was about forty-six years. In a population of about 800,000, over 200,000 children lived on the streets. They survived by getting a noon meal at the houses near where they lived; in return, they protected the neighborhood from children in other blocks.

Carvajal arranged for a number of his business friends to create an informal gathering, which they called the Tuesday Night Club. They met each week to exchange ideas and to consider how they could lead an effort to create a good future for the Cauca Valley, where Cali was located. They made an arrangement with a local university, Universite del Valle, to conduct a mid-career master's program, to which they would send their high-potential young managers. In addition, they developed a program for themselves with the university.

They developed a list of the priority changes for the region—hospital management, public health, education for farmers, communication system needs—and organized into change management teams to make the changes happen in their regions. In addition, each of the members brought an organizational change problem to work on during the educational program. Members made contact with other sectors of the society (labor, regional government, and so on) and enlisted some of them in their classes. The program was quite successful. The hospital in Cali was overhauled, providing more bed space so that patients did not have to stay in the halls, more nurses, and an updated food service. One of the members instituted new personnel policies in his factories, resulting in better working conditions. Several alliances were made between companies.

Carvajal and his friends felt the process was important enough to warrant the effort to try it on the national scale. He enlisted the aid of two universities in Bogota and of the Colombian Management Association, whose efforts the Ford Foundation was supporting. Ford's man on the ground, R. K. Reddy, had been an adult educator and was familiar with MIT and my work. He put together a group of business, government, and academic leaders and asked me to do a one-day seminar on change for his group. My task was to get people enthused and committed to addressing the challenges and opportunities for country development and to provide input on how to manage the change effort. From that, Carvajal and others created a program called Operacion Desarollo (development)— an educational intervention. For eighteen months, the members of one class—two of the president's staff, three cabinet ministers, twenty-five business leaders, the three top labor leaders, and (the second time around) the bishops of the Catholic Church—went to school every Saturday to learn management; we went down to teach them our subjects. Although the various sectors didn't normally talk to each other, they could work together on this educational effort. They could apply what they learned in their own way to their institutions without crossing boundaries. As I taught, it occurred to me that the strength of the change effort hinged on the fact that it was educational and had a neutral subject. If the same people had attended a class on basket weaving or learning to fly an airplane, the same dynamic would have occurred. Management was a process and was content-free. They could, therefore, work on that, even though they could not seem to work on anything to do with the political or social situation of their country.

We conducted the program twice. After the program it still seemed impossible for the various sectors to cooperate officially; they simply did not interact. Then we created an alumni association that started having alumni meetings, which any graduate could attend. It was a widely known but unpublicized fact that for several years much of the business of the country took place at these alumni meetings. The program and its alumni association were generally credited with making a fundamental difference in the collaboration between sectors of society to do what was best for the country.

Our change goal had been to improve communication between the leadership of the major sectors of the society. We reasoned that this would increase people's capacity to use their own and the country's remarkable natural resources. Cooperation between the leadership could help Colombia develop a viable economy and improve societal conditions. We had stumbled upon perhaps the most effective means of getting a fundamental change to happen: an educational intervention. Participants were committed to learning about management because it would be useful to their function. They were all there to learn; their outside roles were irrelevant. In the course, it was useless to engage in political and power struggles: there was nothing to struggle over. As I soon learned, whatever the issue or the country, education is key.

Bridges in Denmark

In 1964, Freddie Jepperson, one of the top managers of BP Denmark who had been a senior executive in 1963 at Sloan, asked me to give a speech to the business leaders of Denmark in Copenhagen. The speech went well and I received offers to make similar speeches at various other associations, including the association of engineers and the management association. Initially, I was impressed with my popularity; then I learned better. In Denmark, the various trade and professional associations were responsive to a Ministry of Trade and Industry, or of Education. The associations could receive funding from the government for training activities. This funding supported the rest of their efforts such as lobbying and member service. The various associations all had to fulfill programs and were hungry for speakers. They kept their speaker lists private, just as two consumer companies protect their patents and products. It was taboo for the training people in one agency to cooperate with their counterparts, so the competition for speakers continued.

One evening, I discussed this no-win situation with John Hendrickson, the human resources head of BP. We also discussed my change model and the strategies for getting commitment. He and a couple of colleagues suggested creating an educational institution that was a nonorganization. From this, the Danish Association for Commercial and Industrial Education (DACIE) was born. Its meetings were held once a month in a hotel dining room. To be a member, one simply came to the meeting. No substantive decisions could be made. The only organizational role was that someone agreed to arrange for the next meeting. The public purpose of the group was professional development for training people. DACIE was a tremendous success, allowing all kinds of bridges between people.

Two years later, we developed an OD program for the country. We held one week-long program and two three-day programs at the Hamlet Hotel in Eisinore, Denmark. I was the outside dean. I recruited Bill Dyer as another professional. Three other experienced OD people completed the faculty. DACIE sponsored the program, and it was DACIE's official nonexistence that enabled all the competitors to attend. One of the universities agreed to take in and disperse the money. From this program, the field of OD emerged as a profession in Denmark. Three years later, when I was doing a workshop with the BP leadership from three Scandinavian countries, Hendrickson and his colleagues arranged for an evening with OD consultants to meet with the executives attending the workshop. Forty-five consultants, all with active practices, attended. The sheer size of the gathering was a wonderful bit of feedback on what had been an enormously successful educational intervention.

Educating to Go Global

I had been consulting with the top management and the personnel leadership of Imperial Chemical Industries for several years when the company began changing its definition from that of a multinational to a global company. This meant all sorts of changes, ranging from the practical questions of where the global board should be located to establishing new methods for managing the matrix between product management, territorial management, and functional management. It also meant establishing global personnel policies. With the decision to go global came a number of questions of governance and management, all involving major changes in relationships, communications, information management, and human resource policies. Within ICI, there were a number of divisions or businesses, most of which were the largest companies in their industries. The semiautonomous division CEOs were faced with monumental issues that were quite new to them.

John Harvey Jones was ICI's deputy chairman at that time. He and his board colleagues were deeply concerned about the organization's capacity to manage these fundamental changes. In earlier years, when he was a division CEO, I had done some work with him on managing change. Now he felt that there was an urgent need to upgrade the skills of the division "boards"—the executive managers of the divisions—to manage these complex changes. My internal counterpart suggested that using my change model could be helpful, and I was asked to conduct a change workshop. I recruited Ed Schein, my friend and colleague, and we designed a three-day workshop. The main concept of the design was to help the managers use a model for planning and managing a major change effort. The participants found the workshop helpful, and we had numerous requests to conduct similar programs for division executive teams. I was also asked to do another workshop six months later.

Ed Schein was unable to participate in the second workshop because of schedule conflicts. In his place I recruited two organization consultants from the company to work with me as staff, with an eye to their conducting future workshops. The second program was equally successful.

The workshop soon became a core part of the training activities offered to managers by the central personnel office. It was generally credited by officers and managers as being a significant influence in increasing ICI managers' process awareness and problem-solving skills. It also had an effect on relationships between organization levels. There were major changes in the location of decisions and the degree of participation and commitment to change among middle and first-line management.

An Education in Israel

Yoram Zeira, a faculty member of the School of Management at Tel Aviv University, spent a semester as a visiting professor in the organization studies group at the Sloan School in the late seventies. At the end of his stay, he asked if I would be interested in visiting Israel to conduct some seminars with their faculty and perhaps a public change workshop and a seminar for social scientists.

A year later, this invitation turned into reality. In 1980, under the sponsorship of the Management School at the University of Tel Aviv, I conducted a two-day workshop, attended by eighty of the key figures in the country, including the heads of several government agencies, the Council of Kibbutzen, the educational leadership, two political leaders from the Knesset (parliament), and leaders of various social sector agencies (health and social welfare). I used my change model to help them learn; we used their change issues as case studies as they worked through the model. I also conducted a seminar on organization change and complexity management for social scientists, academics, and consultants. The following year, Zeira and his colleagues asked me to do some work with the executive council of KOOR, the Labor Party's business arm, rather like a national association of manufacturers.

Major learnings for me from these assignments were about the culture and people of Israel. Of more personal significance, I found myself feeling at home there. The feelings were similar to those I had experienced when visiting Ireland. But I understood feeling connected there, for I knew my mother was of Irish descent. I had not expected such experience in Israel. My religious training as a child had been one of convenience and logistics. My paternal grandfather had been one of the founders of the Ethical Culture

Society, an ethical alternative religion; my father had attended the Ethical Culture High School. I had never been told that my paternal grandfather had been raised Jewish. Discovering this connection was a profound, almost epiphanic, experience.

Fourteen years later, I went back to Israel to do some work. My wife Sandra (my third and current wife) went with me. Sandra had grown up in Wisconsin in a Protestant setting. Her father had been raised Jewish. Based on my 1980 experience, I thought Sandra might feel some connection. I was right, but I had no idea of the impact. During that trip, she met and stayed with some of her Israeli friends and some of mine. She learned all that she could about the Jewish tradition. The following year she returned to Israel to read a paper about communities, and she visited a number of kibbutzim. Sandra has continued her interest in Judaism.

Missionary Orientation Program

As I discovered, educational interventions can be effective strategies for change in large systems of any variety. In a departure from my typical work, I used educational interventions to help missionaries from ten Protestant denominations become better prepared to cope with the realities they would face in the field.

Reverend Donald Smith, the head of the missionary program in the Presbyterian church, had attended a workshop of mine on conference planning. We talked a lot at the conference and afterward about a problem the church was having with its missionaries. Their casualty rate, the percentage of people who could not complete their first assignment and had to be brought home, was alarmingly high. Because the missionaries had all undergone several months of training before they left, we looked at that training to see how it might be improved. The curriculum included ecumenical studies, Bible studies, and some community development studies, mostly through presentation of materials, discussions, and readings. We decided to try a radically different, experience-based program.

We designed a six-month work-study program that built upon my understanding of experience-based learning. One of the basic blocks in our design was to induce the type of stresses, from housing to cultural differences, that the missionaries might find on their assignments. Our hope was that the staff could help the missionaries understand diversity and stress in the training period rather than when they got overseas and had no support.

In the first week, we set up small groups of candidates with the goals of assigning spouses to different groups and achieving heterogeneity. Most of these young people were a bit naive, relying on the fact that "they had been called for this work" to deal with all the issues. We knew we had to create stress situations to test their adaptability. The only rule in the first week of T-groups was that participants could not pray. This was traumatic for them, since with this one stroke, we removed their role protection. We included work on influencing and consulting and on a work project (two of which were building a church in Harlem along with volunteers from the congregation and recruiting white members for an all-black church on the south side of Chicago). By the time candidates graduated, the missionaries and their families were prepared for some of the cultural stressors they would face in their assignments. They had learned about cultural differences and had at least begun the process of changing their attitudes from that of converting the heathens to partnering with non-Christians in the development of their own lives. In addition, they had increased sensitivity to other cultures and to people's different roles in life.

We all had learnings from this experience. For me, they included learning how

- To become a group member, when you had only yourself to offer

- An understanding of process can be applied universally, regardless of content

- An acceptance of cultural differences is essential in developing a community, both geographically and spiritually

- Learning through feedback on present behavior is essential for growth—whether growth in a person, a group, or an organization

Another major learning for me was that learners must be in charge of their learning. The role of the teacher, consultant, or supervisor is to create the conditions that make that possible and to provide support as needed.

The environment and support we offered was clearly helpful. As a result of this program, the casualty rate of the missionaries and their families was dramatically reduced. It went from about 30 percent to a little over 10 percent.

Yet another series of educational interventions was also concerned with casualty rates, though in a different sense. Over the years, I was involved in numerous interventions pertaining to the medical field and medical education in particular.

Interventions for Medical Education

Some of the most dramatic examples of my use of the educational intervention as a change strategy occurred in medical education, both in the United States and abroad. I worked with the Martin Luther King Health Center in New York, projects associated with MIT in Boston, and interventions in the United Kingdom.

Martin Luther King Health Center

My connection to the Martin Luther King Health Center came through my longstanding relationship with Margaret Mahoney, one of the most important people in my life, both professionally and personally. I met her in the Washington, D.C. airport one day in 1972, as we were both flying back to New York. She told me of some work she was funding in neighborhood health centers through her role as program director for health programs at Carnegie. The Carnegie Foundation was funding a social experiment, a neighborhood health center in the South Bronx called the Martin Luther King Health Center. It was an outreach program that had been spun off from Montfiore Medical Center and was then headed by Dr. Harold Wise.

Wise was a remarkable man. He was a visionary thinker and doer and a genius in social experiments. He had developed a new form of care delivery—family-oriented and team-based. The delivery teams were composed of internists, pediatricians, nurse practitioners, advanced nurses, family health workers, and residents of the community who were the point of contact with the patient families in their neighborhoods. Wise believed that anyone could become competent in 60 percent of what a doctor does in six months, and he instituted a training program for people in the neighborhood who wanted to become family health workers. The institution, with a staff of 500 and a patient population of 25,000, was making a significant difference to life in the Bronx. The people were doing great work, but the organization was full of problems in internal communications, decision making, clarity of responsibilities, and collaboration between deliverers and administrators.

Mahoney told me that Wise needed some help in the management of the center; she urged me to work with him. The foundation would pay me. I demurred. I had more than enough on my plate, and I thought I couldn't take on another time-consuming client. Nevertheless, in her own special way, she set up a meeting for me in her office with Wise.

She was right. That was the beginning of a thirty-year relationship with Harold Wise. Today he is my primary doctor and has saved my life a couple of times. In the beginning of our relationship,

I consulted with him and his senior staff at MLK. Together, we brought some order into the management. We established communications policies and mechanisms, performance criteria, and some structural design.

Social Medicine as a Field

Wise was also heading a new residency program at Montfiore in social medicine. Residents in pediatrics and internal medicine could choose to specialize in this new field, which was similar to but different from community medicine and family practice specialties.

Wise had developed a curriculum that included a study of family dynamics, personality theory, learning theory, and change management theory and practice. He felt that the effective physician in social medicine was a change agent for both patients and community. I was an adjunct to his faculty, teaching the postgraduate doctors how to be change agents. I brought in an MIT colleague, Irvin Rubin, and we developed a course in team building and effectiveness for the residents.

Growing from the residency program, Wise, some key students, and I created the Institute for Health Team Development, which Margaret Mahoney funded. A few years later Wise left the program for other pursuits. Jo Boufford and Suzanne Eichhorn took over the direction of the institute. Subsequently, Boufford became a White House Fellow, and Eichhorn became a VA Fellow. They both have continued to have national and international influence on health policy. Boufford is currently assistant deputy secretary in the U.S. Department of Health and Human Services; Eichhorn has an extensive consulting practice with major health leaders.

Educational Interventions to Improve Medical Care

I was impressed enough with the power of educational interventions that I started an educational research project at MIT called Educational Interventions in Improving Medical Care to study the effect

of educational interventions on delivery units. I recruited a staff—
a faculty colleague and three Ph.D. students—to work with me. We
recruited fifteen health policy and delivery professionals, from whose
affiliations we could select field sites for our study. In return for their
willingness to participate in the study, at no charge to them, I conducted a custom-designed ten-week version of my fifteen-week
change management course for them. Our staff selected three sub-
projects: a neighborhood health center, a nursing school, and the
nursing department at Massachusetts General Hospital. In each of
these field sites, we created an intervention using educational methods to facilitate a major change. The course was seen as helpful, and
the research produced some useful findings.

At that point, Margaret Mahoney was vice president of the
newly founded Robert Wood Johnson Foundation, second only in
size to the Ford Foundation. I had the honor of receiving their first
grant, which covered three years' funding for the project.

AAMC Management Advancement Program

I was also involved in the Johnson Foundation's second grant. The
Association of Medical Colleges is the "trade association" for the
medical education world. Through a matching system of applicants
and schools, it administers the admission process for all medical
school candidates in the United States. It is a powerful lobby in
influencing both the training of medical students and the clinical
and scientific research, most of which is done in medical schools.
Its members include all the academic medical centers and all the
teaching hospitals. These constituencies are represented by councils—the Council of Deans and the Council of Teaching Hospitals
being the principal ones.

Most of the financial support of the operation of a medical
school comes from grants for both education and research. The
National Institutes of Health had been the primary funder of the
research and ensured the school's survival. Management needs were
minimal. The department chairs ran their departments. The dean

handled overall administration, including connections with the universities of which they were a part.

During the Nixon administration in the early 1970s, the NIH funding dried up. Medical school deans were now required to manage the multi-million-dollar enterprises they headed. But most of them had little experience and not much interest in organization management. Deans were "elected" by the faculty of the school and had such power as the faculty gave them; a dean's tenure was often as brief as three years.

The Council of Deans had realized the necessity for management skills for deans. They had previously commissioned the management school in a university to conduct a program in management for new deans. The program, which had focused entirely on the human relations skills of managers, had been a disaster. The teaching method had been inductive, using sensitivity training techniques. Now the executive committee of the council was searching for another way of bringing management training to the new deans. The staff director of the council was Dr. Marjorie Wilson, who was the director of the institutional development division of the AAMC.

She had applied for and received a grant from Margaret Mahoney to conduct a management course for new deans. Margaret suggested they talk to several management professors, including me, for advice and help in planning the course. I shocked them by saying I thought they ought to change the project from a course for new deans to an overview of management theory and practice for present deans. I acknowledged their concern about the lack of management skills of many of the deans and suggested that they call their planned series of conferences with teams from schools to work on improving their management Phase Two. Before putting that into operation, they should create a Phase One, a one-week overview of management theory and practice course, whose purpose would be to expose the deans to the field and provide an opportunity for them to discuss with management experts the application to the management of medical schools. I told them that the two most needed areas for such a program were the management of planning and the management of people. Subjects should include strategic planning, management control, and accounting for nonaccountants. In the people area, subjects should include communications, team effectiveness, intergroup relationships, coaching and consulting, and change management.

They needed to find a management school where the faculty specialists from the different disciplines could collaborate on the design. In my opinion, the two faculties of major schools that already worked that way were the Stanford Business School and the Sloan School at MIT. They chose MIT, largely because Dr. Irvin London, who had been on the executive committee of the council, was on the faculty.

I urged them not to let any faculty have free reign to design and conduct the program. They, the executive committee, would need to commit time during the following summer to jointly plan the program. In addition, they should have one of their members attend all subsequent sessions to monitor the quality and the applicability of the content. Their function in the planning process would be to reality test the theories and concepts the faculty would present. I also told them to insist that the program remain under their control, not the management school's.

They agreed to my suggestions, and the program started that fall at Endicott House, MIT's Conference House in Dedham, Massachusetts. Marjorie Wilson was the overall head of the program; Ed Roberts was the faculty dean of the program, and I was co-dean. There were two major themes in the week: managing planning (which Roberts covered) and managing people (which I covered). The first year we did the program twice; after that, annually. Over the years, all of the 104 United States medical school deans, plus a few from Canada, attended the program, about 24 to each session.

That program became the AAMC Management Advancement Program and continues in some form to this day. I stayed with it for about ten years and watched it grow from a program for deans to a program for teaching hospital administrators. The feedback created enough interest that several associations of specialists chose to have us conduct programs for them. The first such group was made up of the pathologists, then the radiologists, then the association of departments of internal medicine. The Council of Surgeons ran an independent program, using a different format.

Out of the MIT one-week program, which they labeled Phase One, the AAMC set up a Phase Two. Three or four times a year they conducted a three-day workshop for teams from four medical centers. The deans, who must have attended Phase One, would determine who they wanted to join them from their institutions for the three days and what issues they wanted to work on during the workshop. The teams from each organization were the core of the program. We supplemented this with content input (about a third of what we presented in Phase One). The staff also served as organization consultants to the work teams.

This educational intervention was generally credited by the AAMC leaders and members and by the management teams of the institutions as effecting significant change and improvement in medical school curricula.

Medical Interventions in the United Kingdom

I also worked for fifteen years in medical education projects in the U.K. My first such project was with the Kings Fund College, which was then heavily involved in management education for the National Health Service. I participated in their general management training for a number of years, conducting two-day sessions on the management of change and complexity.

I also helped develop a change fellows program in the NHS, through the creation of an NHS Training Authority. My task was to work with the program to develop managers into change consultants, to be a curriculum adviser, and to conduct change workshops for the fellows at the beginning of their two-year training. Again, the target was to equip them to function as consultants in organization change.

Learnings and Teachings on Large Systems Change

After participating in several major change efforts, I felt the need to develop some theory about education and large systems change. I discussed this with colleagues who I knew had similar experiences with interventions. At that point, I was teaching at Sloan and wondered what one would teach a person who was planning interventions in large complex systems—and how one would teach it.

Learning from the CIBA Conference

Early in 1977, I had participated in a CIBA Foundation writing conference in London. The foundation, which was concerned with the health and medical fields, had developed a process for writing a book in two days. To do this, they brought together a group of experts on some clinical or public health issue (examples included treatment medicine and the changing roles of nursing). The one I attended had to do with national health policy; I had been invited because of my work with the AAMC and the Kings Fund College.

Theirs was a fascinating format. A subarea of the main topic was presented. Harold Bridger, who was chairing the conference, called on two or three people to present papers. This was followed by a one-hour discussion involving everyone in the group, all of whom were experts in their fields. The entire process was recorded. During the breaks, staff members interviewed all participants, asking them about their remarks and thinking. Staff then processed participants' comments. Two weeks later, each participant received a document in which was recorded anything he or she had said to the interviewers and in the discussions, along with the context around the remarks. We were asked to edit this and return it to the staff.

Six weeks after the conference, a hard-cover book appeared. The process and the speed were remarkable.

Leading the Writing Conference

I hit on the idea of staging a writing conference whose topic was teaching large system change. I invited twenty-five human resource managers and academics from the United States, Latin America, and Europe to join me for two days at Endicott House in August of 1977. Once there, we were to address two questions:

- What should be the content in teaching large system change?

- How would we design different venues (a graduate course, a public workshop, an in-house workshop, and so on) for teaching this content?

Everyone I invited agreed to attend. I was able to get funding from the industry participants that allowed the academics to travel to the conference. MIT covered the housing costs.

After dinner on the first day, we went into the lounge for coffee. Marv Weisbord sat down at the piano and began playing; soon we were all standing around the piano singing and requesting favorite tunes. I consider that evening as instrumental in creating the climate of cooperation and creativity in the group. The second day was a quantum leap ahead of the first in terms of productivity. As a result of the conference, we produced two working papers that are available at MIT: "Core Content of the Teaching of Large System Change" and "Explorations on the Teaching and Learning of the Managing of Large System Change" (see Resource A). We chose not to publish a book at that time. Subsequently, I wrote an article titled "The Writing Conference: A Mechanism for Technology Transfer" describing the experience and our findings (see Resource A). That article is still in wide use.

Impact of Interventions

As I developed my model of change and applied it in several settings, I became convinced that educational interventions were a powerful way to get a major change achieved in a complex institution. I had seen some dramatic results in the Colombia project, which had changed the country, and in school systems and industrial organizations. The varied educational interventions with which I have been associated have moved participants and teachers forward. We have all been changed by them. I have, I hope, learned in each of them, whether I was consulting with senior managers on large system change projects, teaching and coaching practitioners and leaders on management change, or acting as a consultant to effect a significant, often transformational, change in a system. And primary among those systems were the family and the family business systems with which I reconnected at various points in my career.

9

Developing a Field

Consulting with Family Businesses

In the early eighties, I was operating at peak. I was teaching in the master's, Ph.D., Sloan Fellows, and senior executive programs at MIT. I was committed to regular visits to Procter & Gamble in Cincinnati and to ICI, Lyons, and HCA in London. I was staffing a program at Bethel each summer, while living in my family home on Lake Kezar and writing a book.

Again, as at the beginning of the seventies, I was busy, happy, and fat. And again, a sense of unease appeared. Everything I was doing had been fully tested and required little initiative. I was giving a lot but not learning very much. My activities in the health field were no longer central. My consulting practice was stable, as was my teaching at MIT. What next? As it happened, it was time to revisit family businesses, where my career had begun.

Returning to Family Businesses

My first consulting clients had been small, family-owned businesses. In fact, my consulting practice had grown from one client, Robert Hood at Ansul Chemical Company, to several clients, including George Raymond and the Raymond Company, and Roger Sonnabend, president of the Hotel Corporation of America, where I had a ten-year retainer. It was a consulting and learning experience. Like Hood, both of these clients were second-generation heads of family businesses. This pattern continued when I picked up work in Europe: my first clients there were large multinational, family-controlled businesses. In time, my practice changed so that my principal clients were large public organizations. But my interest in and connection to family businesses was revived in the mid-seventies when I reconnected with George Raymond and the family business.

My research and teaching assistant, Gibb Dyer, had met Raymond when he was a visiting client in the practicum course. Gibb was doing research on cultures, including family business cultures; Raymond invited him to visit the Raymond Company and do some field research.

It was then that I consulted with Ivan Lansberg, who owned a large insurance conglomerate in Venezuela. About the same time, I was also asked to consult with Bernardo Garcia Vega, the CEO of a very large conglomerate in Monterey, Mexico—Grupo Alfa. In both cases, the initial request was for help in top team management and organization structure. The work quickly became consultation to the CEO personally, and our discussions focused on the tensions between their multiple roles of being owner, CEO, and head of the family.

Developing a Field of Study

In searching for what was known about family businesses, my teaching assistant, Gibb Dyer, and I became aware that there was almost nothing on family businesses in the literature. There was virtually no attention being paid in management courses or research to the unique issues of family businesses. With one small exception—an "institute" and a small program at the Wharton School, University of Pennsylvania, under Peter Davis—no courses were given that we could find. Instead, business and management schools were training students to become senior managers in General Motors or IBM, a future that did not mesh with reality. In the United States at that time, almost 95 percent of all businesses were family owned or controlled. Even more startling was the fact that 173 of the *Fortune* 500 companies were in this category.

As I digested these figures, I realized the massive disconnect between the focus of our teaching design and reality. This was reaffirmed with a study of the Sloan student body indicating that over 70 percent of the entering master's students came from family business families. Upon entering the program, many, if not most of them, did not intend to enter the family business; by the end of their second year, three-quarters had changed their minds and were preparing to enter the family business.

I saw an opportunity for my next few years. I designed a process for transferring research findings in management, specifically management of family-owned businesses. I based this on a program I'd seen at the University of Michigan in which some members of an institute faculty recruited a group of CEOs to participate in and fund a program. I contacted several of my former clients and explained the project and its possible value to family business leaders. I asked them to contribute to funding a three-year action-research project; the funds were to cover Gibb's salary and other expenses; I contributed my time. I also asked that they make their companies available as field sites for our research. I was delighted that everyone I contacted agreed to participate. We had one founder, two second-generation presidents, and the professional CEO in a large family-owned business. One member came from Canada, two from the United States, one from Mexico, and one from Venezuela.

The first year, Gibb and I reviewed what research there was. We interviewed a number of owners and identified issues they would find helpful to address. According to our contract, we would present our findings to the group at a meeting at the end of the year. The group could react to the data, identify the relevance for their own companies, and identify other issues we should explore, using their organizations as field sites.

In preparing for the first meeting, we analyzed the research and identified some key issues. We wrote several articles for the *Sloan Management Review*, including "Managing Change in the Family Firm," as well as a working paper titled "Challenges and Issues in Managing Family Firms" (see Resource A).

Warner Burke, who was then editor of *Organizational Dynamics*, asked me to put together an issue of the magazine devoted entirely to family business issues. I produced the issue entitled "Managing Continuity in the Family Owned Business" (summer, 1983). Authors included Gibb Dyer, Ivan Lansberg, Jr., and Harry Levinson. I included an article, as did my wife Elaine, who was a Gestalt and a family therapist and who had presented some family dynamics at the first group meeting of the sponsors. The fact that the issue was well received by the subscribers and had an impact on the group I was working with affirmed my feeling that there was an important field of study and practice waiting to be developed.

At the end of the second year the group met again to hear some further inputs and to share experiences. At this meeting, they queried us about other research, education, and consulting that was going on. When we identified the few active programs, they prodded us: "Why don't you people talk to each other?" That got me thinking about the need for some professional development in the field. Perhaps a network of people doing research or consulting, perhaps a professional development course such as the program for specialists in organization development (PSOD) that I had created at NTL in the late sixties. We wanted a safe setting (akin to the one DACIE had established), where people could talk and learn from each other.

Elaine and I got excited about the idea of developing a workshop for practitioners that could cover the content we had discussed in the MIT program but from the point of view of a family business consultant. We discussed possible content and designs. We thought we might be able to create an institute to present some relevant courses. Perhaps we could develop the courses in the summer near our home in Maine.

We looked for a facility, but anything we liked was out of our reach financially. The following winter, Barbara Hollander, who was a friend of Elaine's, visited us in New York. She was a family therapist and had a successful practice in Pittsburgh, consulting with families that owned businesses. Over drinks, we discussed our interest in the creation of a professional training institute. Barbara was enthusiastic about the idea and eager to do something about it. She offered to join us in a design and agreed to be the active project manager. By the time we sat down to dinner, we were committed to moving ahead, to creating the Family Firm Institute.

The Family Firm Institute Is Born

We decided to start by offering some courses and creating an organization. By our rough estimates, we hoped to get going with capitalization of $10,000. We each agreed to put up $2,000 and to recruit friends for the other $4,000. Ivan Lansberg, Jr., George Raymond, and Alan Levinson, a CEO and client of Hollander's, became stakeholders. We designated ourselves the founding board of the Family Firm Institute and scheduled a founding meeting in Elaine's and my apartment in New York. Our business members made the formal and legal arrangements.

We defined the Family Firm Institute as primarily a professional education organization; members would be consultants from several disciplines who worked with family business clients. There would be three program areas: an annual conference with an educational emphasis, study groups for regional meetings and sharing, and a journal. The journal would include research, concept, and practice articles. It would not be a purely academic publication, requiring referenced articles; neither would it be a slick magazine. We allocated assignments to ourselves. Barbara Hollander became president; Elaine was project head in developing the study group program; Ivan Lansberg was the journal editor; I led the team on conference planning.

In the summer of 1984, John Davis had convened a research group for a family business conference at Santa Barbara, where he was on the university faculty. Ivan, Elaine, and Barbara attended, with the goal of explaining the new FFI and recruiting attendees to join. Most of the attendees agreed to participate in the first FFI annual conference to be held the following year. This was a big success: this critical mass of professionals in the field lent legitimacy to our conference. Nancy Drosdow of the Center for Applied Research at the University of Pennsylvania offered to host the meeting in Philadelphia. I helped her and was one of the keynote speakers. Forty-five people attended; we all thought it an impressive size. That conference set the precedents for future formats.

Study groups were formed in several areas of the country, as we had agreed at the founding meeting. Ivan Lansberg proceeded to develop an editorial advisory committee for the journal. I was able to negotiate a deal with Jossey-Bass Publishers to underwrite the production costs and handle promotion. Under this arrangement, FFI would totally control the content and would receive a royalty on all sales.

Following my pattern of leaving something when it matures, I resigned from the board at the end of my first term. Then, for another two years, I consulted with the new board that was elected. A few years later, the organization hired a part-time executive director, and I moved out of any active leadership role. I continued to participate actively in the conferences: I spoke at several of them and presented workshops at others.

Today there is an FFI office with two full-time staff members, including a professional executive director. The organization's activities include the annual conference, the *Family Business Review* (the journal), a newsletter, and a number of seminars and workshops. The group can be contacted at 12 Harris Street, Brookline Massachusetts, 02146 (617-738-1591). A subset of the membership has developed an Association of Family Business Forums, a network of universities that have family business programs, institutes, and forums.

The original group of family therapists and OD consultants has been augmented by family business lawyers, accountants, and insurance consultants. The total membership was roughly 1,000 in 1996; over 400 of those members attended the annual conference, "Power Up the Family Business," that year. For me the whole development of the field has been thrilling. From a project envisioned in the minds of a few of us has emerged a powerful institution that continues to benefit its members.

Moving On

And so I had come full circle with family businesses: they had been the start of my consulting work, and I helped form an organization that would continue to benefit their leaders. As I eased out of active consulting I began to look for other ways in which I could give back to the fields in which I had worked, to organization development in general, and to the community at large.

10

Adding Value, Senior Style

Over the years, I helped a number of clients think about and plan career and life transitions. When the clients were heads of family businesses, the connection between career and family was very clear—and something we discussed often. Life transitions also came up in meetings with other clients, consultants, and students.

I have described my professional transitions from theater to laboratory trainer, to meetings and education consultant, to OD consultant, to organization consultant, to university professor throughout this book. Personal transitions occurred with the death of my first wife after a thirty-two-year marriage and with my separation and divorce (in 1987) from my second wife, Elaine Kepner. Not all of these transitions were part of the clear career plan that I had in mind for myself by the late sixties. I expected: to continue to teach at MIT until my retirement age, which I would reach in 1984; to continue consulting with a few clients around the world with whom I had open-ended arrangements; to continue at NTL, focusing on professional development programs; and to continue writing and editing. On the personal side, I expected to still be married to my first wife.

I have learned through experience and the experiences of those I have consulted and taught that the correlation between a good plan and a good outcome is, to say the least, unreliable. This helped me to understand and explain to myself why so many organizations' strategic plans don't end up in effective actions. It also helped me reconcile the fact that although some of my plans worked out, several didn't.

I did retire from MIT in 1984. My consulting work had developed, but it did not last as long as I had anticipated. I had planned for an orderly transition from half-time professor and half-time consultant, to occasional adjunct professor and mostly consultant. I followed this plan. After my retirement from MIT, I taught one course on change in the graduate school of Teachers College, Columbia University, in 1985 and 1986. In a separate contract, I was an adjunct faculty member of their certificate program for senior-level human resources managers, called organization development and human resource management (ODHRM). I began participating in this program at its inception in 1976 and continue to spend a day a year in it. I was also recruited to be an adjunct faculty member on the Pepperdine University master of science in organization development (MSOD) program and have taught in that course since 1976 as well.

Writing became more powerful in the mix of my activities and identities. Harris and I wrote a second edition of our book, *Organization Transitions*. I continued to coedit, with Ed Schein, the Addison-Wesley OD series. In time, an identity that I hadn't anticipated became the core of my practice in the nineties, but first I had to make a transition of my own.

A New Age

As the bells rang in the New Year of 1990, I was facing a combination of challenges I had never experienced. My income had halved, and was about to halve again. I was living alone for the first time in fifty years. It had been more than a year since my open-heart surgery and I felt pretty good, but knew I would have heart disease as long as I lived. There was not too much work on the horizon.

I thank the good Lord for my innate optimism. I felt, down deep, that things would be all right. I had enough income from royalties, Social Security, and a small MIT pension to cover my basic needs. The financial consequences of my divorce made it very difficult to maintain my overhead expenses, but I believed that I could generate enough consulting income to manage. And I did receive calls, asking me to speak somewhere, do a workshop, meet with a top team, shadow consult somewhere. But it was not a lot.

Then, before I could really become concerned, a "divine intervention" occurred. A friend called me to say that her college roommate from Wellesley some twenty-five years previous was visiting before she went back to California. Her visitor was considering a career in OD; would I talk with her? I agreed, and we made an appointment for a Tuesday.

In our two-hour meeting, I advised her not to go into OD. The field was too crowded with younger, better-trained people; I thought she would have a very difficult time. During the last twenty or so years, she had taught in a school for children, worked with the elderly, and worked in a law office.

Hers was an interesting story. She seemed like a warm, nice person. I gave her the names of some people she could contact if she wanted to seriously pursue going into OD. I took her to the elevator and said goodbye and went back to my office to do some "important" work.

Two hours later I was hit with what felt like a bolt of lightning. I knew I wanted to spend the rest of my life with this woman. This feeling made no sense to me, a Taurus, a feet-on-the-ground type. I was even experiencing physical symptoms: my face was flushed; I began to perspire. Perhaps I was coming down with the flu. I skipped dinner, took two Tylenol, and went to bed knowing that everything would be all right in the morning.

It wasn't. The feeling was still there. I had to get in touch with Sandra. She had mentioned that she liked jazz; her husband, who had died the year before, was a well-known jazz trombonist. I called my friend and invited them both to join me for dinner and listening to jazz at a club in my neighborhood on Friday night. My friend couldn't make it. She was teaching in the evening and going out of town later but suggested that Sandy might like to go. After some cliffhanging no's and maybe's, Sandy agreed to meet me for dinner and jazz. We have not been apart since that night.

Sandy is a wonderful, warm human being. There is a twenty-five-year age difference, but we both feel like peers. She has become my best friend as well as lover and companion. Her presence has made me feel younger, not older. My physical health is the best it's been in twenty years, according to my doctor. My personal life had taken a dramatic turn; how would my professional life fare?

Coaching Becomes My Identity

For the one day a year I spent with the participants in the Teachers College program, I had created a design in which I spent the morning in a general session, talking about change, and the afternoon, working for one hour with each of the four learning teams.

Every participant brought a change case to the program. In preparation for the working session, the team selected one case. I would work with the presenter as a consultant, looking at the intervention strategy and asking questions, using my change model as a guide. The team would then spend the rest of the hour identifying the learnings from the consultation, led by their core faculty member.

David Nadler, founder and CEO of the Delta Consulting Group, a major management consulting firm, had been one of the core faculty at several of these sessions. A few years later he asked me to attend a retreat of his professional staff, to demonstrate the technique I had used with a couple of their ongoing cases. The consultants found this useful. I entered into an arrangement whereby I visited Delta once a month. On that day, I was available to discuss "cases" with anyone who wanted to book time. I realized

that I had found a new niche: I could provide coaching and counseling to professionals. I recalled from my theater days how all
singers and dancers, regardless of their fame or achievements, used
coaches. The same is true for golfers and tennis professionals. Why
not consultants?

Coaching Consultants

My first clients were some of the Delta consultants. Several other
practitioners I knew asked to get coaching help. The practice
extended to the point that, together with counseling clients, coaching consultants represents more than half of my work. Currently
about a dozen consultants come to me for coaching, in much the
same way professional singers or dancers work with coaches but
without the same rigid schedule.

A pattern began to emerge in these consultations. The consultants' stated reason for wanting to talk with me was to have a "fresh
perspective" and check with a senior person on some of their work.
We would start with discussing their case. As we discussed their role
issues and intervention strategies, the focus would almost always
change to more personal questions. As they got more comfortable
in discussions with me, they would share their need to talk with
somebody about their career and life plans.

In almost every case they disclosed that they were not fully
happy with their present situation and where they were going in
life. In some cases they were frustrated with the lack of stimula-
tion they were getting from their practice. Others felt they were
not at the level of hierarchy that they felt they should be; some
felt unappreciated from the top. Several were considering moving
to smaller, single-person or partnership practices. A common com-
plaint was that the demands the work and their company were
making on them caused havoc in their family life. To my surprise,
the consultants were not primarily concerned with financial security, or even with maximizing projected income. They were making a good living. What was bothering them was their personal

fulfillment and happiness and, in several cases, their contribution to society.

As but one example, Richard was a senior associate in a large consulting firm where he had been for three years. He was bringing in over $500,000 a year in fees. He was doing very well financially. To service his clients, he was working about ninety hours a week. He was traveling an average of three and a half days a week. He was in the office for nonclient meetings at least one day a week. He worked an average of three evenings at home, where he had access to e-mail and computer conferences, which were frequent. He tried to be with his children on weekends but was less than successful in meeting this goal. The children wanted to know where their father was; his wife was concerned about their relationship.

As we talked, Richard's conflicts became clear. He was ambitious and wanted to become a millionaire. He liked the work, even though it was very demanding. He was also a strong family man; helping his children develop was a high priority. He was torn apart by the two demands—from the firm and from the family—and was unable to see how to change the balance of his life.

I pushed him to define what he liked about his work and what was less meaningful. He liked having a long-term relationship with a few clients, where trust could be developed and he could help the client in a more holistic way than was possible under the ground rules. I proposed that he fantasize a completely satisfactory practice. He said that he would have one, or at the most two, major client relationships. Servicing them would take about 40 percent of his time. He was very interested in writing a book and wanted to spend 30 percent of his time writing. He also wanted to take a couple of courses for his own professional development.

I asked him to develop a strategy and a plan to put that scenario into place within a year. He discussed our meeting with his wife. She enthusiastically supported the scenario. He made the plan, left the firm in which he worked, started his own small private practice. A year later he had his clients; his income was just about the same as a year before. The family was in great shape. He was a different person; the stress lines in his face were gone. He was a success—and by his own accounting.

In this case and in others, some of what I do could be called "shadow consulting." My description of it, and one that the clients agree with, is that it's like a coaching session. I try to help clients with their own strategies, concerns, and goals.

Empowering People Under Stress

An unusual part of my practice was initiated by my primary doctor and friend, Harold Wise, with whom I first worked at the Martin Luther King Health Center. Wise is a competent, board-certified internist whose approach is to treat the patient holistically. He has assembled a first-class team of specialists to whom he refers his patients as necessary. Today, his is a "Park Avenue" practice; many of his patients are professionals, entrepreneurs, artists, and senior public servants. Some of his patients exhibit stress syndromes but do not need psychiatric help. They do not need a psychologist or a career counselor but something in between, and Wise refers them to me for a form of career counseling. It is an unusual practice in which I am fortunate enough to help people, usually interesting people, become renewed and empowered to manage their current life transitions.

I have developed a specialized format for such interactions. I see the "client" only one time, for sixty to ninety minutes. The model I use, based on many previous discussions and studies about empowering people, relies on two concepts: the theory of structural tension and the theory of energy.

According to the theory of structural tension, there is a pull toward achieving a goal (a change) and a pull toward maintaining the status quo (no change). These two forces are connected with a metaphorical rubber band, producing tension. If one starts toward the goal and finds it is impossible to continue, it is usually because the pull to no change (the status quo) is stronger than the pull to change (the new goal). In this case, the status quo pole pulls harder; it shows reasons why you can't do what you want. Since the status quo tends to be stronger in many people's minds, they react by not taking chances. If, on the other hand, one believes or can be convinced that the pull toward the future is stronger than the status quo, the balance shifts. Then, when one starts toward the goal and experiences pressure not to continue, one can treat that pressure as a hurdle to be jumped over rather than an obstacle that blocks progress. In this case, the journey toward the desired state continues. It does not stop, and it does not take an unplanned detour.

The other theory that I use is a theory of energy. Energy itself is neutral. People under stress are expending vast amounts of energy, with a negative direction. This causes them to turn inward, feel powerless, and become confused. An amateur "cure" suggests reducing the stress, perhaps by taking a vacation or lying on the beach. Reality is that those who follow that prescription may take their problems to the beach—and they may also get sunburned.

Instead, in my work with clients, I treat energy as an asset, much as I did in my confrontation meeting model (see Chapter Six and Resource C), which has been used successfully by hundreds of organizations. If the energy is negative and headed in the wrong direction, the goal is to turn it around in a positive direction. I apply the "hourglass" theory: if something isn't working, turn it 180 degrees in the opposite direction and see what happens. In essence, I treat negative energy as an asset that is currently aimed in the wrong direction and therefore in need of a 180-degree turn. The system—whether an individual or an organization—needs to be put under tension to reach short-term goals. The often-used word for this is *positive tension*. Imagine the rubber band part of a slingshot. In order to successfully shoot the pellet, the rubber band must be back far enough to get force into the shot. Too far and it breaks; too slack and there is not enough force to achieve the objective. Applied to the clients' situations, the idea of positive tension requires setting explicit and demanding short-term goals (often one year) that demand energy to achieve. The clients must develop the commitment to expend that energy, to pull the band far enough to project themselves into their desired future.

As part of the session I would often have people "dream" what would be a perfect situation a year from now. It might mean a change of workplace; it might mean starting their own company. Occasionally clients exposed their real, often long-buried, dreams for themselves. Susannah, who was a competent amateur pianist, did just that by acknowledging that she had always wanted to become a professional pianist. We explored what it would take for that to happen. I helped her develop a plan to get there, including activities needed. From this, she saw that it would be possible to move toward her dream while still supporting herself. She changed jobs, took on some piano teaching, and began her move.

Another client's desired change seemed, on its surface, to be less drastic. Valerie had been in the advertising business for a number of years. She was a successful executive. Her work was interesting and demanding. She did her job well and was financially rewarded. She believed in and practiced professional and personal development. A course that she attended in organization development was a powerful experience for her, so powerful that she decided to make a career shift. The values and practice of OD seemed to her a better fit than her present world. She came to see me, to discuss how she could start a practice. From professional issues our agenda moved to the more personal questions and how to synergize the two.

One of her ex-agency clients had a big divisionwide meeting coming up. They asked if the agency could help stage the meeting. One of the executives recommended that the client talk to Valerie. From that talk came a contract to help design the meeting and to support the management. This led to a series of other projects with the same client. Through word of mouth, she also acquired two other large clients and now has a successful practice. I functioned as a shadow consultant for her early interventions. After her skills and confidence were well developed, she did not need my support.

In consulting clients, I have seen incredible results and an exciting success rate. Over thirty clients have had experiences similar to the ones I just described; more than 75 percent of them take positive actions and report back progress and clear directions for next steps in their lives.

I have learned that if you can create enough positive tension, short-term goals, and pressure to reach them, people can do amazing things. People leave after an hour, changed and committed, and they follow up! I credit the profound change to their becoming aware that negative energy can be an asset if turned in a positive direction. The process releases the energy that has been holding them back: people get new energy and can really turn around. It is very personally satisfying to me to have been a help in their empowerment. I have also had the good fortune to coach on a different scale through master classes.

Exploring Master Classes

In the eighties, I had become involved with the Kings Fund College, a research and training institution, in London. They conducted a number of training programs for the National Health Service, including some for senior management. I was asked to conduct a workshop on change as part of their senior management course. I also was asked to consult with the director of the college on both program and institutional issues.

In the course of this, I met Greg Parston again; I had worked with him in the early eighties when he was the planner and vice president in an Academic Health Center in New York and I was consulting with the president. Greg had moved to London, where he had become a fellow (senior faculty) at the Kings College. After a few years in that role, the director had appointed him as his deputy.

Greg Parston was convinced that there was need for expanding management awareness to the entire public sector leadership. But the directorate at the college was reluctant to move beyond the health areas. So in 1980, Greg and another senior faculty member, Laurie McMahon, created a new organization called the Office of Public Management. The purpose of the organization was to provide consulting and training services to departments and agencies whose mission was to create a better social sector, a better society, through getting social results. Their clients include the National Health Service, the U.S. Department of Education, the chief executives of local authorities, and the police.

Parston and McMahon asked me to advise them in setting up the organization. They continued to consult with me on the governance of the group and on the establishment of institutional norms and ground rules. They set up the Public Management Foundation, a nonprofit entity, to conduct research on issues of managing the social sector and to conduct public conferences on related subjects, including change management and organization development. They invited me to become a trustee (the equivalent of a board member) of their foundation. In that capacity, I made speeches on their behalf at conferences, and I conducted workshops and seminars for them. After a few years, I joined the staff as a senior visiting fellow. In that function, I spend a week, once or twice a year, in London. Parston and McMahon schedule my time and activities. I consult with them and with the board of directors. I conduct internal change workshops for staff, consult on educational interventions, and shadow consult some of the consultants, much as I do in the States.

In the early nineties, Greg asked me to conduct some master classes in organization development for senior health managers. Master classes were first created for the performing arts, where they are used with some regularity. They are workshops for professionals, who want some coaching from a "master." For example, Pavarotti might conduct a master class for professional singers. Parston saw that the concept had wider application, that it was directly applicable to organization management. Together, we designed a master class for senior health managers. That was the first of many such classes. Under the auspices of the Office of Public Management (OPM), I have conducted master classes for local authority chief executives, education department executives, police constables, and health managers.

I have used the concept outside of OPM as well. For instance, I gave a master class for senior partners in a large consulting firm. I gave one in the United Kingdom for the leaders of the change practice of one of the Big Six accounting firms. I did a class for OD practitioners at a recent OD network conference to demonstrate the process.

Using My Experience to Facilitate Learning

My professional activities in these years are a direct reflection of my two goals—(1) to influence large systems to be more effective and more human and (2) to help in the development of the next generation to continue that process. In most of my career, my "work" was in the first goal. My professional responsibility was acted out in the second goal.

Today, in my later years, this has been reversed. My "work" is in helping the development of others. To keep my hand in the real world, I do some large system consulting and counseling for chief executives. I continue my editing of the Addison-Wesley OD series, and I continue to write. My rewards come largely from my interactions and joint learning with colleagues. These keep me growing and looking toward the future.

11

Looking Back and Ahead
Learnings and Legacies

Certainly, I have lived a rich life. There is much that I have learned in the past forty-nine years, so much that I've felt an obligation to my mentors, clients, and students to give something back for what I have gained. My hope is that reading of my learnings will be useful to students and practitioners of organization change and development in their personal and professional lives.

In this chapter, I attempt to integrate my learnings about consulting, about being a change agent, about learning and teaching, and about transferring knowledge and experience through writing. I attempt to distill some of my knowledge and experience, what wisdom I've accumulated on my journey, and to put it to paper.

Transitioning to the Future

I have experienced an incredible period of history. I have traveled by horse-drawn buggy, automobiles, airplanes, and the Concorde. My first radio was a crystal set; today my computer is connected to the Internet. In Maine we once did all our cooking on the woodstove; now we have a microwave. Yet my experience of change will seem pale compared to what people half my age will experience.

The rate of change in this information age rises exponentially. Everything in the world is potentially accessible to everyone in the world. New products such as computers and cellular telephones become obsolete in two years. Electronic gadgets come on the market daily. It makes my head spin. But keeping pace with the changes is critical: advances in technology have had and will have a profound effect on the way we do work, on how organizations organize, and on how we manage our home life.

Alongside these technological changes, there is a vast social upheaval. Questions that must be addressed include: What will be the new balance between the private, public, and the social sector? Will wealth be developed solely from the private sector, or will the social sector be a source of producing wealth through jobs? How can organization leaders determine their local, national, and global markets? How will they decide in which markets to operate? How do we deal with the issues between the developed North and the developing South? How do we deal with issues such as poverty, AIDS, and reforestation?

Practically all major businesses, foundations, churches, education systems, and social agencies are reexamining their missions. They are redefining and repositioning their place in the scheme of things and deciding how they will organize in the repositioned state. All of these changes in communication, services, and manufacturing will require behavior changes by executives, managers, workers, and consultants. As agents of change, the opportunities for us to make a contribution are unlimited. We bring skills in managing complexity and the change process. Through our research, teaching, and consulting, we provide a unique capacity to help the decision makers in organizations and institutions determine their futures.

I am often asked what the future holds for OD. My typical response—OD as we know it is dead—surprises people. But as happens when nature renews itself, OD is seeding the future of organization change and development. In a sense, it's already reinventing itself. It is clear that thriving organizations in the next millennium will operate with team management. The complexity of the world makes any other management strategy suspect. OD consultants, already skilled in managing organizational processes, bring a major contribution to making teams effective. Indeed, who better to guide the transformation to team management than the OD experts?

The work to be done will define how we organize to do it. And rightly so. Shouldn't form follow function after all? No longer will the pyramid structure, or any other single structure, be relevant. Decisions will have to be made at all levels of the organization in ways that we could not have dreamed of twenty years ago, based on where information comes together. Here we have the makings of an OD intervention. Organizations will be designed differently. Organizations will operate in multistructures defined by tasks. In keeping with this, the concept of staff-line will be replaced by that of performer-supporters. The management of the operation of an institution will still be by the line functions such as sales or manufacturing or the staff functions such as finance and human resources. But formal roles such as sales manager and manufacturing manager will move from fixed responsibilities to fluid states. The management of defining and planning the future state of the organization will be in the hands of the strategic planners, the information managers, and the human resource leadership. Flatter structures, managing information, applying technology—all these are changes from present practice that OD consultants can facilitate. Organization development expertise will play a critical role in the management of change. Managing conflict and complexity will become even more central. For these reasons, the employment market for OD practitioners is the best it has ever been. Large management consulting firms and Big Six accounting firms are recruiting at full speed for both client work and internal development and can be expected to continue to do so. OD's technology and experience is now being sought after as never before. Is the field ready?

Re-Tooling Strategies

Most of the institutions connected to OD emerged since 1950 and are now maturing. NTL will be fifty years old in 1997. Back in 1995, it embarked upon a major review process, reexamining its mission, programs, identity, and values. It is today a vital institution with a wide array of workshops and offerings. The Pepperdine MSOD program celebrated its twentieth anniversary in 1995 and made a fresh commitment to proving a critical mass in influencing social change. Instead of "relaxing" in their stability, the leaders of these institutions and programs are deeply involved in the process of reinventing and repositioning themselves. There are several new graduate degree programs in OD. Certificate programs such as ODHRM are booming, in spite of the national trend by industry to cut down on outside training programs.

The professional training in OD and change seems to have passed through what might be called its mid-life crisis, when innovation and creativity were at low ebb. Now there is a new burst of energy and sense of power that is exciting to see.

In parallel with the transformation of the field of OD, in the past few years I too have gone through a transformation. I have come to redefine my work as primarily supporting other practitioners, coaching people, and writing. Paradoxically, this transformation has been triggered by celebrations of the past. The celebrations and the process of writing this book have made me reflect deeply on who I am, what I have been and done, and what I want to leave as my small contribution to a better world.

My basic identity has been as a change agent. As a consultant and coach, I've worked with family-owned businesses, the leadership of national and multinational business organizations, foundations, churches, social services organizations (such as the Red Cross and the Girl Scouts), and community organizations, universities and colleges, and school systems. As a trainer, I have done human relations and leadership and change management training, in both public and in-house settings, for organizations and associations in the United States, United Kingdom, Canada, Mexico, Netherlands, Norway, Denmark, Finland, Australia, and the Republic of Ireland. I have taught university graduate courses at MIT, Columbia Teachers College, Case Western Reserve University, Pepperdine University, and the London Graduate School of Business. As a conceptual model builder, I have devised

- A model of managing change

- An open systems planning model

- The confrontation meeting

- A model for planning workshops and conferences

- A commitment planning model supported by responsibility charting

- Educational interventions to achieve change in complex institutions or organizations

In my coaching of consultants and in teaching master classes for consultants, I have passed on these learnings. In all of these functions, I have relied on my ability to conceptualize, strategize, and create bold ways of attacking issues. I have been recognized for contributing ideas, for mentoring action leaders, for designing interventions, and for monitoring systems. But even before (or without) the recognition, I enjoy and get strong internal rewards from empowering others, be they clients, students, or colleagues. Much of my work is bringing together people, groups, and institutions to produce both a synergy and better products. I rather like thinking of myself as a catalyst.

What advice would I give to people—consultants, change agents, teachers and counselors, coaches—who are playing any of the roles I have played in my career?

Advice to Consultants

Consultants are—or should be—value adders. As a consultant, it's important to remember that you do not own the problem; the client does. The value you add is to increase the client's capacity to solve the presenting issues and any others that you might subsequently agree upon. You are not there to have your needs met.

A key to your effectiveness is your capacity to empathize—to get into the client's head and see the problem from that perspective. A second critical factor is your capacity to listen to the music, to understand the meaning behind the words. Relaxed listening (think of yourself as a sponge), particularly during the client's presentation of the problem, allows you to access and use whatever experience you have that is relevant to the interaction.

Try to make every relationship a joint inquiry or learning. The standard organizational roles—client, consultant, CEO—will only get in the way. Keep the power balance in the client's favor. Deal with the natural dependency that exists whenever one asks for help. At the beginning of a relationship, by asking for expert help, the client is giving the consultant power. To add value, ask questions, push clients to define their goals, remember that the problem is the client's.

Advice to Change Agents

Understand that you are an *agent* of change, not a manager of change. Manage the pressure to own the problem or to be part of the management. Focus on managing dilemmas rather than solutions. Provide leadership in diagnosing problems and in suggesting processes for diagnosis. Provide systems thinking as a way to gain perspective on problems. Look at the system and the relationships of the parts. Be clear about who the client(s) are: they may be the entry clients, the CEO, the top team, the human resources department, or others. Be clear with all clients about your own values, principles, and practice methods. For example, I always make it crystal clear that I will not be a message carrier; I respect confidentiality with all clients.

In open-ended relationships, build in a condition that either party can terminate at any time. But be sure that all parties recognize that major change takes time and that premature closure should be avoided.

Be prepared for multiple relationships with the same person or group—consultant-expert, counselor-educator. Understand and communicate the education part of your role. Get feedback from all clients.

Focus on listening to the client's music, what is behind the words, what the client is really telling you or asking you. Then you will be in a better position to hear the truth. If instead you are focused on your own position, strategy, or security, you are likely to close off getting in touch with all the knowledge and experience that is in you. Trust the process and you will find, perhaps to your surprise, that you can access other experience and apply it to the current situation.

Advice to Teachers

Through developing my model of teaching and learning as a transactional situation, I revised my concept of "teacher" from one who transfers knowledge and skills to others to one who creates the conditions for students to learn and, in the process, learns as well. Remember that despite the title, a teacher's key role is to create the conditions for learning, not to teach. All learning is transactional, and all learning is change. Define learning goals for a course or a program that include the level of learning-change, knowledge, understanding, attitude, behavior, and skill.

Set up the format for the course or program so that you can learn, both in the design and the conduct of the activity. Be sure to get and use feedback from your students and from other teachers.

Advice to Counselors and Coaches

I have realized over time that in either a teaching or consulting relationship, the student or client owns the problem—the teacher or consultant does not. A metaphor that helped was to think of myself as a coach or athletic pro. A football coach designs the plays, helps the players with their skills, and then watches from the sidelines as they perform. A golf pro provides the learner with the rules of the game, helps the learner develop skills, and guides practice. Once the learner starts playing, the pro's role is to coach. The coach provides an educational intervention that causes the players or students or clients to develop more capacity to manage change and development. So, as a counselor or coach, your primary mission is to increase clients' effectiveness. You must use your experience and knowledge in helping clients access their goals, hopes, and fears.

It helps to keep the relationship professional and periodic. Present opportunities and possibilities for the client to consider. Encourage the client's dreaming and visioning. This may mean providing crazy ideas and other interventions that stretch the client's thinking. For example, I have suggested to several organizations that they create their own university and fold their training into it; this moves them away from traditional training programs and roles.

Encourage and reward clients for progress in both confidence and competence. As clients make changes in their behavior or their management of the process, I try to give them feedback on the effectiveness of their actions, either through objective data or by passing on reactions from significant others in the organization or system. The client's success is the consultant's reward. As a theatrical director, my reward was seeing the work I had done come to life on stage; the audience didn't—and didn't need to—understand my contribution. Similarly as a consultant, my reward is the internal satisfaction I derive from seeing clients absorb ideas and take significant actions.

More Advice

Some pieces of the advice I'd give people in my various fields pertain across the board. No matter what the function you're taking on—consultant, change agent, counselor, or coach— first you need to manage yourself. You must be sure that your needs and wants are met without eclipsing the needs of those you are intending to help.

This can be the most difficult part of the job. Often there is a deli-cate balance between

- Needing the job and staying objective

- Needing billable days and doing a quality job

- Being honest with clients and pleasing them

- Feeling competent and acting competent

- Advising clients and learning from them

- The role of expert and the role of consultant

- Needing to control and needing to help

As consultants, we must manage a variety of internal and exter-nal demands. It's important to remind ourselves that consultants are there to add value, to help the clients, not to control them. With our expertise, it may be appropriate to control the process instead.

Talking about fees can be uncomfortable, but don't make the mistake of letting it slide. Work out the fee arrangement at the beginning. Review it periodically. Don't wait for the client to say, "What's the fee?"

The client's willingness to pay your fee gives you some feedback on the value of your work. Be sure to build in other feedback as well. Without specific feedback, your value to the client is limited, and your growth for future clients is halted.

Wherever possible, give the clients choices among alternative strategies or decisions—and describe the consequences of each. Allow openings for the client to volunteer alternatives beyond those that you describe and help the client to analyze all the options presented.

Last, take special effort to manage the tension between a busi-ness and a personal relationship with clients. This can be especially tricky and needs to be managed on a case-by-case basis. Consultant and client must both be secure enough in their professional relationship and trust each other enough to allow any friendship to develop alongside the professional relationship and not impinge upon it. If the relationship ever becomes muddied, it helps to specify which role you are playing during an interaction, perhaps by explicitly saying, "I am wearing my consultant's hat when I say. . . ."

The Past as Prologue

I have always believed that one doesn't retire from the kind of career I had. This belief was affirmed a few years ago when I spoke with John Garner (former Secretary of Health, Education, and Welfare; adviser to six U.S. presidents; founder of Common Cause; and respected author and scholar), who was then in his eighties. He told me that the word *retire* wasn't in his vocabulary. He would go on being active until the end of his journey. Being active meant thinking ahead, using past experience as a basis for future thinking. It's a challenge, and one that I've taken up. That is the excitement of the times for me.

I am currently involved in significant repositionings of a number of organizations, including NTL, a church institution, two foundations, and a consulting-training institution in the United Kingdom. I am functioning as an adjunct in several professional development programs that are attended by the future leaders in the field. I am an advisory board member of the Peter F. Drucker Foundation for Non-Profit Management, whose mission is to expose the leadership of the nonprofit sector to the best in managing thinking and practice. I am one of three editors of a series published by Jossey-Bass called The Drucker Future Series, a collection of essays by leading academics, writers, management consultants, and organization leaders. The first book—*The Leader of the Future*—came out in June of 1996. The second book, *Organization of the Future*, was published in December of 1996. A third book, *The Community of the Future*, will follow at the end of 1997.

Several themes, or consistent perceptions of the future, have appeared in the first two books:

- Thriving organizations will have team leadership. The unique tasks of the top leaders will be to make the team leadership effective.

- Decisions will be made and managed close to the problem and based on knowledge, not status.

- Information management will become the province of the top management and line management; it will be a core part of strategic management.

- The nature of the functions to be performed will determine the make-up of teams to manage them. The single bureaucratic structure based on authority will be replaced by a multistructure dedicated to different classes of tasks.

- Lifetime company loyalty by employees will be replaced by a strong sense of interdependence among employees and their leaders. Functional managers will probably have more loyalty to their professions than to their companies.

- Managing dilemmas will be a primary skill for leaders and managers.

- The organization will be an open system. Stakeholders will include employees, unions, boards of directors, stockholders, the media, and the community. Healthy organizations will have social agenda in addition to economic agenda.

- Innovations and creativity will be among the top criteria that will measure the success of a management.

- More and more company policies and practices will be values-driven. Economic goals will still have to be met, but for the organization to stay at the leading edge, attention to values is required.

There also seems to be agreement that in the millennium, the social sector of our society will become increasingly potent. We can expect the social sector to be the biggest provider of jobs, surpassing the private and public sectors; this represents a major change from present conditions. The line between volunteer and paid work will blur as more people work part-time or are part volunteer, part paid. Some boards of directors already reflect this: some are paid, some are all-volunteer, some have a mix of members.

All of these changes will require effort and thought—thought by which we can benefit by putting in today. In all my endeavors, and in this book, I hope to stimulate people's thinking about their professional work and its intersection with their personal life. My professional and personal lives have certainly meshed in a way that continues to be full and stimulating; may yours as well.

Resource A

A Chronology of the Works of Dick Beckhard

Books

Changing the Essence: The Art of Creating and Leading Fundamental Change In Organizations (with Wendy Pritchard). San Francisco: Jossey-Bass, 1992.

Organizational Transitions: Managing Complex Change (with Reuben Harris). Reading, Mass.: Addison-Wesley, 1977.

Making Health Teams Work. Cambridge, Mass.: Ballinger, 1974.

Organization Development: Strategies and Models. Reading, Mass.: Addison-Wesley, 1969. (Also coeditor with Warren Bennis and Edgar Schein of the remaining volumes in this nine-volume series on organization development.)

Conference Planning (ed.). Selected Reading Six. Washington, D.C.: NTL Institute for Applied Behavioral Science, 1970.

The Leader Looks at the Consultative Process. Looking into Leadership Series. Washington, D.C.: Leadership Resources, Inc., 1961.

How to Plan and Conduct Workshops and Conferences. New York: Association Press, 1956.

The Fact-Finding Conference (with W. Schmidt). Adult Education Association of the USA, 1956.

Chapters in Books

"From Confusion to Fusion: Integrating Our Educational and Managerial Efforts." In E. Schein, *The Art of Managing Human Resources.* New York: Oxford University Press, 1987.

Note: Items are arranged in reverse chronological order.

"The Executive Management of Transformational Change." In R. H. Kilmann,
T. J. Covin, and Associates, *Corporate Transformation*. San Francisco:
Jossey-Bass, 1987.

"Applied Behavioral Science for Health Organizations" (with N. Tichy). In
M. Margulies and J. Adams, *Organization Development in Health Care
Organizations*. Reading, Mass.: Addison-Wesley, 1981.

"Organization Changing Through Consultation and Training." In D. Sinha (ed.),
Consultants and Consulting Styles. New Delhi, India: Vision Books, 1979.

"Managing Behavioral Factors in Human Service Organizations" (with
N. Tichy). In *Management Handbook for Public Administrations*. New York:
Van Nostrand Reinhold, 1979.

"Stratefien zur Veranderung Grobber Systeme." In B. Sievers (HRSG), *Organisa-
tionsentwicklung Als Problem*. Stuttgart, West Germany, 1977.

"Managerial Careers in Transition: Dilemmas and Directions." In *New Perspec-
tives in Organizational Careers*. London: Wiley, 1976.

"Short and Long Range Effects of a Team Development Effort" (with D. Lake).
In H. Hornstein and W. Burke, *Social Intervention—A Behavioral Science
Approach*. Free Press, 1971.

"Organization Development in the U.S.A." In F. Balvig (ed.), *Organization
Development in Practice*. Copenhagen, Denmark. 1971.

"OD as a Process." In *What's Wrong with Work?* New York: National Association
of Manufacturers, 1967.

Articles in Periodicals

"Comments on 'When the Computer Takes Over the Office' by I. R. Hoos."
Office: Technology and People, 1984.

"Managing Continuity in the Family-Owned Business" (with W. Gibb Dyer).
Organizational Dynamics, 1983 (summer), *12*(1).

"Conversation with Richard Beckhard" (by I. Lansberg, Jr.). *Organizational
Dynamics*, 1983 (summer), *12*(1).

"Managing Change in the Family Firm." *Sloan Management Review*, 1983, *24*(3).

"SMR Forum: Managing Change in the Family Firm—Issues and Strategies"
(with G. Dyer). *Sloan Management Review*, spring 1983, *24*(3).

"Responsibility Charting: An Alternative to Crippling Power Struggles." *Trustee
Magazine*, Apr. 1981.

"Who Needs Us? Some Hard Thoughts About a Moving Target—The Future."
Keynote speech, *OD Practitioner*, Dec. 1981.

Review of *Interactions and Interventions in Organizations* by I. Mangham. *Journal
of Applied Behavioral Science*, 1980.

"Teaching Organizational Psychology to Middle Managers: A Process Approach" (with E. Schein and J. Driscoll). *MIT Exchange V*, 1980.

"Dick Beckhard on Managing Change." *Bulletin on Training*. BNA Communications, Inc. July-Aug. 1979.

"Portraits of 17 Outstanding Organization Consultants" (T. Becker and E. Glaser). Human Interaction Research Institute, National Institute of Mental Health Research Project, 1979.

"The Writing Conference: A Mechanism for Technology Transfer." *Exchange, The Organizational Behavior Teaching Journal*, 1978, 3(3).

"The Dependency Dilemmas." *Consultant's Communique*, California State University, Northridge, Calif., 1978, 6(3).

"Commentary on 'Making Systems Healthy.'" *Journal of Applied Behavioral Science*, July 1978.

"Strategies for Large System Change." *Sloan Management Review*, 1975, 16(2).

"ABS in Health Care Systems: Who Needs It?" *Journal of Applied Behavioral Science*, 1974, 10(1).

"Profile of the Perfect Executive." *Cincinnati Horizons* (the magazine of the University of Cincinnati), Jan. 1973, 2(3).

"Optimizing Team Building Efforts." *Journal of Contemporary Business*, Oct. 1972, 1(3).

"The Executive You're Counting on May Be Ready to Mutiny." *Innovation Magazine*, May 1972, 31.

"Organization Issues in the Team Delivery of Comprehensive Health Care." *Milbank Memorial Fund Quarterly*, July 1972, 50.

"Applying Theory Y Assumptions in the '70s." *Performance Magazine*, Nov. 1971.

"The Confrontation Meeting." *Harvard Business Review*, Mar.-Apr. 1967. (Also chapter in H. Hornstein, W. Burke, and others, *Social Intervention—A Behavioral Science Approach*. New York: Free Press, 1971.)

"Factors Influencing the Effectiveness of Health Teams." *Milbank Memorial Fund Quarterly*, July 1970, 1(50).

"An Organization Improvement Program in a Decentralized Organization." *Journal of Applied Behavioral Science*, 1966, 2(1).

"Appropriate Use of T-Groups in Organizations." Association of Teachers of Management (ATM) Occasional Papers, 2. G. Whitaker (ed.). Oxford, England: Basil Blackwell, 1965.

"Helping a Group with Planned Change: A Case Study." *Journal of Social Issues*, 1959, 15(2).

Working Papers Published

"Challenges and Issues in Managing Family Firms" (with G. Dyer). MIT WP
    1181–81, Feb. 1981.

Core Content of the Teaching of Large System Change. MIT WP 1024–78, Oct.
    1978.

Explorations on the Teaching and Learning of the Managing of Large System Change.
    MIT WP 1023–78, Oct. 1978.

"Applied Behavioral Science for Health Administrators" (with N. Tichy). MIT
    WP 8979–76, Oct. 1976.

"Organizational Issues in Managing Curriculum Change" (N. Gaspard and
    E. Herzog). MIT WP, Dec. 1976.

Part I WP 561–71, Sloan School of Management, MIT, Oct. 1971.

University Programs and Health Administration Publication. MIT Sloan School of
    Management paper WA 8979–76, Oct. 1976.

"Planned Change in Organization Systems," published as WP 491–70 by MIT
    Sloan School of Management, 1970.

Speeches and Presentations

"Organization Transformations—Fad or Future?" Keynote address, American
    Academy of Management, Aug. 1984.

"Managing Change in a Complex Society." Address at Polyteknisk Forening,
    Oslo, Norway, Nov. 1981.

"The Changing Shape of Management Development." Paper presented at First
    World Congress on Management Development, London, Nov. 20, 1981.

"Critical Issues in Managing Large Systems Change in the Eighties." Keynote
    speech, American Society of Training Directors, May 1981.

"Organizational Aspects and the Change Process." Speech at Health Services
    Resource Center, University of Michigan, Nov. 1976.

"New Pressures on the Corporation." Speech to Innovation Group, Oct. 1971.

"Management of Team Delivery of Comprehensive Health Care." Paper pre-
    sented as part of a panel, "How to Measure Programs of Preventive Medi-
    cine." Joint conference of Association of Teachers of Preventive Medicine
    and American College of Preventive Medicine, Minneapolis, Oct. 1971.

"Planned Change in Organization Systems." Paper presented at Division 14,
    American Psychological Association, Miami Beach, Sept. 5, 1970.

"From Confusion to Fusion: Integrating the Management and Behavioral Sci-
    ences." Douglas McGregor Memorial Lecture, Oct. 1968; MIT Sloan
    School, 1970.

"An Action Research Approach to Organization Improvement." Paper delivered to the American Management Association Personnel Conference, New York, Feb. 7, 1967.

Videotapes and Training Films

Managing Change in Organizations. Reading, Mass.: Addison-Wesley, 1985.

Managing the Change Process: The Transition State. Seattle: Intermedia, Inc., 1983.

(Four productions) *Matrix Management, Structures for Managing Transitions, Commitment Planning, Responsibility Charting*. AT&T Corporate Policy Seminar, 1979.

Responsibility Charting. Atlanta: AAMC/National Medical Audio Visual Center, 1977.

The Raymond Case. American Society of Training and Development, 1971.

Managing in a Crisis. BNA Communications, Inc., 1970.

Theory X and Theory Y. Parts 1 and 2. BNA Communications, Inc., 1970.

Resource B

Commitment and
Responsibility Charts

What is the minimum commitment required from each player or group in order to allow a proposed change to happen? What is needed of each player or group to accomplish the change? To bring about change, do individuals and groups need to

- Make it happen?

- Help it happen, by providing resources?

- Let it happen, by not blocking the process?

The commitment chart can help facilitate this analysis (see Figure 1).

To use the commitment chart, determine the necessary level of commitment for each player and mark an "O" in the appropriate box. Then indicate that player's present state with an "X." If the X and the O are in the same box, the player has the desired commitment. If not, you have to develop a strategy to get the player from X to O, the required position.

Responsibility charting can help clarify the behavior that is required to implement important change tasks, actions, or decisions. To use the responsibility chart, two or more people whose roles interrelate or who manage interdependent groups first formulate a list of actions, decisions, or activities that affect their relationship.

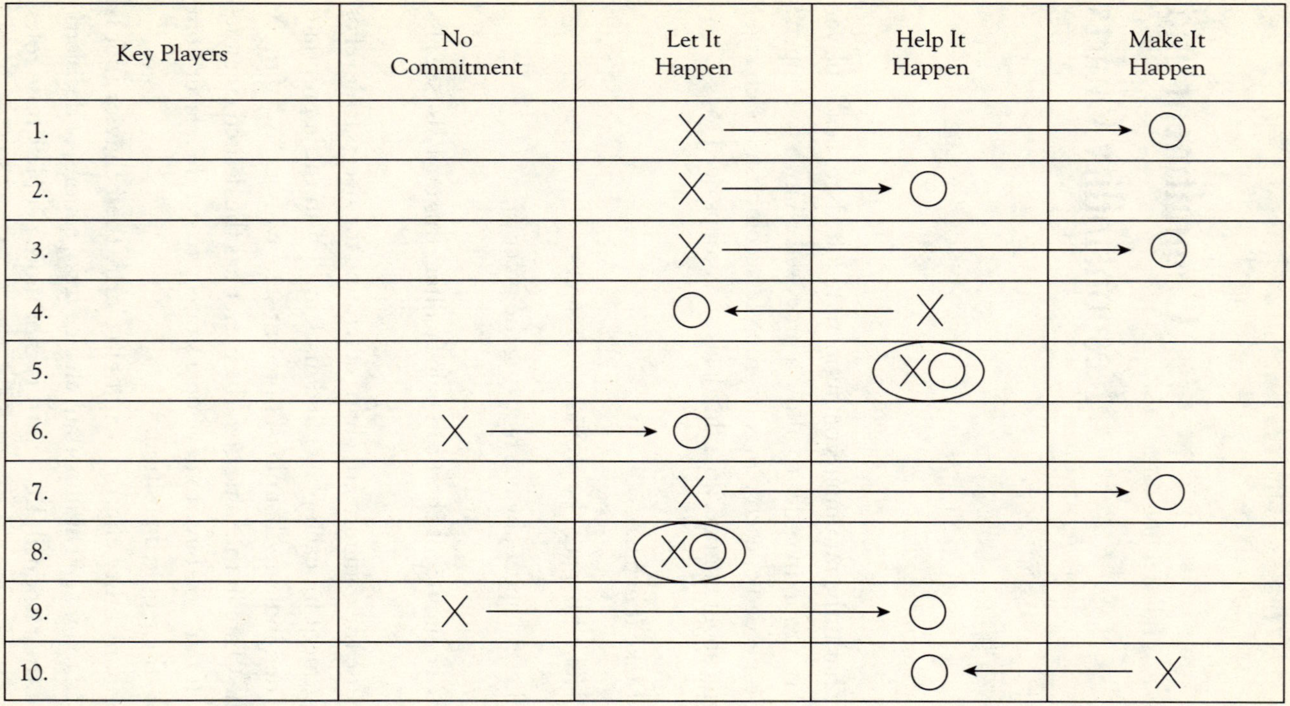

Figure 1. Commitment Chart.
Source: Beckhard and Harris, 1987. Used by permission.

They record the list on the vertical axis of a responsibility chart (see Figure 2).

These actions might include developing budgets, allocating resources, and deciding on the use of capital. They then identify the people involved in each action or decision and list these actors on the horizontal axis of the form. Actors might include those who are directly involved in a decision, the bosses of those involved, groups (boards of directors, project teams), and people outside of the organization (union officials, auditors, bankers). Then the participants chart the appropriate behavior of each actor for each action or decision, using the following classifications:

R   Has *responsibility* for a particular action, but not necessarily authority

A   Must *approve*: has the power to veto the action

S   Must *support*: has to provide resources for the action, but not necessarily agree with it

I   Must be *informed* or consulted before the action, but cannot veto it

-   Irrelevant to the action

Actors					
Decisions or Acts					

Figure 2. Responsibility Chart.
Source: Beckhard and Harris, 1987. Used by permission.

Resource C

The Confrontation Meeting

One of the continuing problems facing the top management team of any organization in times of stress or major change is knowing how to assess accurately the state of the organization's health. How are people reacting to the change? How committed are subordinate managers to the new conditions? Where are the most pressing organization problems?

In the period following a major change such as that brought about by a change in leadership or organization structure, a merger, or the introduction of a new technology, there tends to be much confusion and an expenditure of dysfunctional energy that negatively affects both productivity and morale.

At such times, the top management group usually spends many hours together working on the business problems and finding ways of coping with the new conditions. Frequently, the process of working together under this pressure also has the effect of making the top team more cohesive.

Concurrently, these same managers tend to spend less and less time with their subordinates and with the rest of the organization. Communications decrease between the top and middle levels of management. People at the lower levels often complain that they are less in touch with what is going on than they were before the change. They feel left out. They report having less influence than before, being more unsure of their own decision-making authority, and feeling less sense of ownership in the organization. As a result of this, they tend to make fewer decisions, take fewer risks, and wait until the smoke clears.

When this unrest comes to the attention of top management, the response is usually to take some action such as

- Having each member of the top team hold team meetings with subordinates to communicate the state of affairs, then following this procedure down through the organization

- Holding some general communication improvement meetings

- Conducting an attitude survey to determine priority problems

Any of these actions will probably be helpful, but each requires a considerable investment of time, which is competitive with the time needed to work on the change problem itself.

Action Plans

Recently I have experimented with an activity that allows a total management group, drawn from all levels of the organization, to take a quick reading of its own health and—*within a matter of hours*—to set action plans for improving it. I call this activity a *confrontation meeting.*

The activity is based on my previous experience with an action-oriented method of planned change in which information on problems and attitudes is collected and fed back to those who produced it, and steps are taken to start action plans for improvement of the condition.

Sometimes, following situations of organizational stress, the elapsed time in moving from identification of the problem to collaborative action planning must be extremely brief. The confrontation meeting can be carried out in four and one-half to five hours' working time, and it is designed to include the entire management of a large system in a joint action-planning program.

I have found this approach to be particularly practical in organizations where the management group is large or where it is difficult to take the entire group off the job for any length of time. The activity has been conducted several times with a one-evening and one-morning session—taking only two and one-half hours out of a regular working day.

The confrontation meeting discussed here has been used in a number of different organization situations. Experience shows that it is appropriate where

- There is a need for the total management group to examine its own workings

- Very limited time is available for the activity

- Top management wishes to improve the conditions quickly

- There is enough cohesion in the top team to ensure follow-up

- There is real commitment to resolving the issues on the part of top management

- The organization is experiencing, or has recently experienced, some major change

In order to show how this technique can speed the process of getting the information and acting on it, let us first look at three actual company situations where this approach has been successfully applied. Then we will examine both the positive results and the possible problems that could occur through the use and misuse of this technique. Finally, after a brief summary, I will give examples that show in some detail how the phasing and scheduling of such a meeting might be done.

Case Example A

The initial application of the confrontation meeting technique occurred in 1965 in a large food products company. Into this longtime family-owned and closely controlled company, there was introduced for the first time a nonfamily, professional, general manager. He had been promoted from the ranks of the group that had previously reported to the family-member general manager.

This change in the "management culture," which had been carefully and thoroughly prepared by the family executives, was carried out with a minimum number of problems. The new general manager and his operating heads spent many hours together and developed a quite open problem-solving climate and an effective, cohesive team. Day-to-day operations were left pretty much in the hands of their immediate subordinates, while the top group focused on planning.

A few months after the change, however, the general manager began getting some information that indicated all was not well further down in the organization. On investigation, he discovered that many middle-level managers were feeling isolated from what was going on. Many were unclear about the authority and functions of the "management committee" (his top team); some were finding it very difficult to see and consult with their bosses (his operating heads); others were not being informed of decisions made at his management committee meetings; still others were apprehensive that a new power elite was developing that, in many ways, was much worse than the former family managers.

In discussing this feedback information with his operating heads, the general manager found one or two who felt these issues required immediate management committee attention. But most of the members of the top team tended to minimize the information as "the usual griping," or "people needing too many decisions made for them," or "everybody always wanting to be in on everything."

The general manager then began searching for some way to

- Bring the whole matter into the open

- Determine the magnitude and potency of the total problem

- Give his management committee and himself a true picture of the state of the organization's attitudes and concerns

- Collect information on employee needs, problems, and frustrations in some organized way so that corrective actions could be taken in priority order

- Get his management committee members in better tune with their subordinates' feelings and attitudes and put some pressure on the team members for continued two-way communication within their own special areas

- Make clear to the total organization that he—the top manager—was personally concerned

- Set up mechanisms by which all members of the total management group could feel that their individual needs were noticed

- Provide additional mechanisms for supervisors to influence the whole organization

The confrontation meeting was created to satisfy these objectives and to minimize the time in which a large number of people would have to be away from the job.

Some seventy managers, representing the total management group, were brought together for a confrontation meeting starting at 9:00 in the morning and ending at 4:30 in the afternoon. The specific "design" for the day had the following components:

1. Climate setting—establishing willingness to participate
2. Information collecting—getting the attitudes and feelings out in the open
3. Information sharing—making total information available to all
4. Priority setting and group action planning—holding work-unit sessions to set priority actions and to make timetable commitments
5. Organization action planning—getting commitment by top management to the working of these priorities
6. Immediate follow-up by the top management committee—planning first actions and commitments

During the day-long affair, the group identified some eighty problems that were of concern to people throughout the organization; they selected priorities from among them; they began working on these priority issues in functional work units, and each unit produced action recommendations with timetables and targets; and they got a commitment from top management of actions on priorities that would be attended to. The top management team met immediately after the confrontation meeting to pin down the action steps and commitments.

(In subsequent applications of this confrontation meeting approach, a seventh component—a progress review—has been added, since experience has shown that it is important to reconvene the total group four to six weeks later for a progress review, both from the functional units and from the top management team.)

Case Example B

A small company that makes products for the military had been operating at a stable sales volume of $3 million to $4 million. The invention of a new process and the advent of the war in Vietnam suddenly produced an explosion of business. Volume rose to the level of $6 million within six months and promised to redouble within another year.

Top management was desperately trying to (1) keep raw materials flowing through the line, (2) get material processed, (3) find people to hire, (4) discover quicker ways of job training, and (5) maintain quality under the enormously increased pressure.

There was constant interaction among the five members of the top management team. They were aware of the tension and fatigue that existed on the production line, but they were only vaguely aware of the unrest, fatigue, concern, and loneliness of the middle manager and foreman groups. However, enough signals *had* filtered up to the top team to cause concern and a decision that something needed to be done right away. But, because of the pressures of work, finding the time to tackle the problems was as difficult as the issues themselves.

The entire management group agreed to give up one night and one morning; the confrontation meeting was conducted according to the six component phases described earlier, with Phases 1, 2, and 3 being held in the evening and Phases 4, 5, and 6 taking place the following morning.

Case Example C

A management organization took over the operation of a hotel that was in a sorry state of affairs. Under previous absentee ownership, the property had been allowed to run down; individual departments were independent empires; many people in management positions were nonprofessional hotel people (that is, friends of the owners); and there was very low competence in the top management team.

The general manager saw as his priority missions the need to

- Stop the downhill trend
- Overcome a poor public image

- Clean up the property

- Weed out the low-potential (old friends) management

- Bring in professional managers in key spots

- Build a management team

- Build effective operating teams, with the members of the top management team as links

He followed his plan with considerable success. In a period of one year he had significantly cleaned up the property, improved the service, built a new dining room, produced an enviable food quality, and begun to build confidence in key buyers such as convention managers. He had acquired and developed a very fine, professional, young management team that was both competent and highly motivated. This group had been working as a cohesive team on all the hotel's improvement goals; differences between them and their areas seemed to have been largely worked through.

At the level below the top group, the department and section heads, many of whom were also new, had been working under tremendous pressure for over a year to bring about improvements in the property and in the hotel's services. They felt very unappreciated by the top managers, who were described as "always being in meetings and unavailable," or "never rewarding us for good work," or "requiring approval on all decisions but we can't get to see them," or "developing a fine top management club but keeping the pressure on us and we're doing the work."

The problem finally was brought to the attention of the top managers by some of the department heads. Immediate action was indicated, and a confrontation meeting was decided on. It took place in two periods, an afternoon and the following morning. There was an immediate follow-up by the top management team in which many of the issues between departments and functions were identified as stemming back to the modus operandi of the top team.

These issues were openly discussed and were worked through. Also in this application a follow-up report and review session were scheduled for five weeks after the confrontation meeting.

Positive Results

The experience of the foregoing case examples, as well as that of other organizations in which the confrontation meeting technique has been applied, demonstrates that positive results—particularly, improved operational procedures and improved organization health—frequently occur.

Operational Advantages

One of the outstanding plus factors is that procedures that have been confused are clarified. In addition, practices that have been nonexistent are initiated. Typical of these kinds of operational improvement, for example, are the reporting of financial information to operating units, the handling of the reservation system at a hotel, and the inspection procedures and responsibilities in a changing manufacturing process.

Another advantage is that task forces, and/or temporary systems, are set up as needed. These may be in the form of special teams to study the overlap in responsibilities between two departments and to write new statements and descriptions, or to work out a new system for handling order processing from sales to production planning, or to examine the kinds of information that should flow regularly from the management committee to middle management.

Still another improvement is in providing guidance to top management as to specific areas needing priority attention. For example, "the overtime policy set under other conditions is really impeding the achievement of organization requirements," or "the food in the employees' cafeteria is really creating morale problems," or "the lack of understanding of where the organization is going and what top management's goals are is producing apathy," or "what goes on in top management meetings does not get communicated to the middle managers."

Organization Health

In reviewing the experiences of companies where the confrontation meeting approach has been instituted, I have perceived a number of positive results in the area of organization health:

• A high degree of open communication between various departments and organization levels is achieved very quickly. Because people are assigned to functional units and produce data together, it is possible to express the real feeling of one level or group toward another, particularly if the middle echelon believes the top wants to hear it.

• The information collected is current, correct, and "checkable."

• A real dialogue can exist between the top management team and the rest of the management organization, which personalizes the top manager to the total group.

• Larger numbers of people get "ownership" of the problem, since everyone has some influence through his or her unit's guidance to the top management team; thus people feel they have made a real contribution. Even more, the requirement that each functional unit take personal responsibility for resolving some of the issues broadens the base of ownership.

• Collaborative goal setting at several levels is demonstrated and practiced. The mechanism provides requirements for joint goal setting within each functional unit and between top and middle managers. People report that this helps them to understand "management by objectives" more clearly than before.

• The top team can take corrective actions based on valid information. By making real commitments and establishing check or review points, there is a quick building of trust in management's intentions on the part of lower-level managers.

• There tends to be an increase in trust and confidence, both toward the top management team and toward colleagues. A frequently appearing agenda item is the "need for better understanding of the job problems of other departments," and the output of these meetings is often the commitment to some "mechanism for systematic interdepartmental communication." People also report a change in their stereotypes of people in other areas.

• This activity tends to be a "success experience" and thus increases total morale. The process itself, which requires interaction, contribution, and joint work on the problems and which rewards constructive criticism, tends to produce a high degree of enthusiasm and commitment. Because of this, the follow-up activities are crucial in ensuring continuation of this enthusiasm.

Potential Problems

The confrontation meeting technique produces, in a very short time, a great deal of commitment and desire for results on the part of a lot of people. Feelings tend to be more intense than in some other settings because of the concentration of time and manpower. As a result, problems can develop through misuse of the techniques.

If the top management team does not really use the information from its subordinates, or if there are great promises and little follow-up action, more harm can be caused to the organization's health than if the event were never held.

If the confrontation meeting is used as a manipulative device to give people the "feeling of participation," the act can boomerang. They will soon figure out management's intentions, and the reaction can be severe.

Another possible difficulty is that the functional units, full of enthusiasm at the meeting, set unrealistic or impractical goals and commitments. The behavior of the key man in each unit—usually a department manager or division head—is crucial in keeping suggestions in balance.

One more possible problem may appear when the functional units select a few priority issues to report out. While these issues may be the most *urgent*, they are not necessarily the most *important*. Mechanisms for working *all* of the information need to be developed within each functional unit. In one of the case examples cited earlier, the groups worked the few problems they identified very thoroughly and never touched the others. This necessitated a "replay" six months later.

In Summary

In periods of stress following major organization changes, there tends to be much confusion and energy expended that negatively affects productivity and organization health.

The top management team needs quick, efficient ways of sensing the state of the organization's attitudes and feelings in order to plan appropriate actions and to devote its energy to the most important problems.

The usual methods of attitude surveys, extended staff meetings, and so forth demand extensive time and require a delay between getting the information and acting on it.

A short micromechanism called a confrontation meeting can provide the total management group with

- An accurate reading of the organization's health

- The opportunity for work units to set priorities for improvement

- The opportunity for top management to make appropriate action decisions based on appropriate information from the organization

- An increased involvement in the organization's goals

- A real commitment to action on the part of subgroups

- A basis for determining other mechanisms for communication between levels and groups, appropriate location of decisions, problem solving within subunits, as well as the machinery for upward influence

Example: Confrontation Meeting

Here is a detailed description of the seven components that make up the design for the day-long confrontation meeting.

Phase 1: Climate Setting (45 min to 1 hr)

At the outset, the top manager needs to communicate to the total management group the goals for this meeting and concern for and interest in free discussion and issue facing. The manager also has to assure everyone that there is no punishment for open confrontation.

It is also helpful to have some form of information session or lecture by the top manager or a consultant. Appropriate subjects might deal with the problems of communication, the need for understanding, the assumptions and the goals of the total organization, the concept of shared responsibility for the future of the organization, and the opportunity for and responsibility of influencing the organization.

Phase 2: Information Collecting (1 hr)

The total group is divided into small heterogeneous units of seven or eight people. If there is a top management team that has been holding sessions regularly, it meets as a separate unit. The rest of the participants are assigned to units with a "diagonal slice" of the organization used as a basis for composition, that is, no boss and subordinate are together, and each unit contains members from every functional area.

The assignment given to each of these units is along these lines: "Think of yourself as an individual with needs and goals. Also think as a person concerned about the total organization. What are the obstacles, demotivators, poor procedures or policies, unclear goals, or poor attitudes that exist today? What different conditions, if any, would make the organization more effective and make life in the organization better?"

Each unit is instructed to select a reporter to present its results at a general information-collecting session to be held one hour later.

Phase 3: Information Sharing (1 hr)

Each reporter writes a unit's complete findings on newsprint, which is tacked up around the room.

The meeting leader suggests some categories under which all the data from all the sheets can be located. In other words, if there are seventy-five items, the likelihood is that these can be grouped into six or seven major categories, say, by type of problem, such as "communications difficulties" or by type of relationship, such as "problems with top management" or by type of area involved, such as "problems in the mechanical department."

Then the meeting breaks, either for lunch or, if it happens to be an evening session, until the next morning.

During the break all the data sheets are duplicated for general distribution.

Phase 4: Priority Setting and Group Action Planning (1 hr, 15 min)

The total group reconvenes for a fifteen-minute general session. With the meeting leader, they go through the raw data on the duplicated sheets and put category numbers by each piece of data.

People are now assigned to their functional, natural work units for a one-hour session. Manufacturing people at all levels go to one unit, everybody in sales to another, and so forth. These units are headed by a department manager or division head of that function. This means that some units may have as few as three people and some as many as twenty-five. Each unit is charged to perform three specific tasks:

1. Discuss the problems and issues that affect its area. Decide on the priorities and early actions to which the group is prepared to commit itself. (They should be prepared to share this commitment with their colleagues at the general session.)

2. Identify the issues and/or problems to which the top management team should give its priority attention.

3. Decide how to communicate the results of the session to their subordinates.

Phase 5: Organization Action Planning (1 to 2 hrs)

The total management group reconvenes in a general session, where:

1. Each functional unit reports its commitment and plans to the total group.

2. Each unit reports and lists the items that its members believe the management team should deal with first.

3. The top manager reacts to this list and makes commitments (through setting targets or assigning task forces or timetables, and so on) for action where required.

4. Each unit shares briefly its plans for communicating the results of the confrontation meeting to all subordinates.

Phase 6: Immediate Follow-Up by Top Team (1 to 3 hrs)

The top management team meets immediately after the confrontation meeting ends to plan first follow-up actions, which should then be reported back to the total management group within a few days.

Phase 7: Progress Review (2 hrs)

Follow up with total management group four to six weeks later.

Sample Schedule

9:00 A.M.   Opening remarks by general manager
                Background, goals, outcomes
                Norms of openness and "leveling"
                Personal commitment to follow-up

9:10 A.M.   General session: Communications problems in organizations, remarks by general manager (or consultant)
                The communications process
                Communications breakdowns in organizations and individuals
                Dilemmas to be resolved
                Conditions for more openness

10:00 A.M.   Coffee

10:15 A.M.   Data production unit session
                Sharing feelings and attitudes
                Identifying problems and concerns
                Collecting data

11:15 A.M.   General session: Sharing findings from each unit (on newsprint)
                Developing categories on problem issues

12:15 P.M.   Lunch

2:00 P.M.   General session: Reviewing list of items in categories
                Instructing functional units

2:15 P.M.   Functional unit session: Listing priority actions to be taken
                Preparing recommendations for top team
                Planning for presentation of results at general meeting

3:15 P.M.   General session: Sharing recommendations of functional units
                Listing priorities for top team action
                Planning for communicating results of meeting to others

4:15 P.M.   Closing remarks by general manager
                Adjournment

Index